My Life

in the

Sacred Name Movement

By

Joseph G. Meyer

Introduction

The years are flowing past. I tell my children and grandchildren about the Sacred Name Movement, and our years in it, and I see that they really don't understand. I see historical articles by third parties describing what others have told them, and smile at errors, omissions, and wrong conclusions. I lived through the early formative years of the Sacred Name movement, knew the people, and heard their ideas and discussions off the record. Not many people today are left who have that experience.

This is my memory. Therefore I will make this a work in progress, and I seek correction for any errors of names, facts or misspellings. If you know the people and were there for the events… let's make it accurate! Input is appreciated!

From my earliest years, my life was all about religion. Not because of my efforts, but due to the nature of our family. For over 300 years, the Meyer family has been preachers, teachers, farmers, businessmen, musicians, and scholars. Some in the family have been all of the above at the same time!

My ancestors probably were involved with the Labadist community in Maryland in the late 1600s. They helped to found the Ephrata Cloister in the early 1700s. They helped to build the Church of the Brethren from the middle 1700s through the 20th century. The Meyer family has many entries in the Church of the Brethren histories and encyclopedias.

It should not be surprising that my father, Jacob O. Meyer, would quickly rise to prominence in the Sacred Name Movement. The fact is that he did rise to prominence. Who I am and what I have accomplished is greatly influenced by having worked with him closely, and by having him as a role model.

From my youth, I was fascinated by farming, horses, history, and religion. So, for many hundreds of hours, I sat near my dad, as he talked with the Elders and leaders of the Sacred Name Movement, and heard their discussions, arguments, and Bible Studies. I learned early that I could shadow the Elders, if I was quiet, sat still, didn't pester them, and followed closely in my little Bible.

This is a book of my memories of the Meyer family in the Sacred Name Movement. But I smile when I write that, because my memories are about our family, led by my father, the assembly my father was the leader of, and of many thousands of hours of working with my father, talking with him, traveling with him, reporting to him, studying with him, and helping him. I hope you enjoy this peek into the past through this history of my life in the Sacred Name Movement.

Furthermore, I beg your indulgence on two counts: First, when I stray to share more personal family details, forgive me, because I believe they will help the reader to understand the human nature of our family, and Elder Jacob O. Meyer. Secondly, I have no intention of scandal-mongering. If I mention any details about anyone in this book that offends, I beg your forgiveness. I will at all costs avoid the negative and the critical, but if I fail in that, in any way, forgive me.

Table of Contents

Chapter 1

Searching: 1959-1963

The Meyer Family: Jacob W. Meyer, Jr.

Our family was Church of the Brethren. I won't spell out every position of leadership that they held over the past 250 years. The COB history books will tell that story. There are many references to my Great – great grandfather, Jacob Wenger Meyer, Jr. He was a leader in the community near Fredericsburg, Pa, operated a large farm, was on the board of directors of the Bank, and was President of Elizabethtown College.

J. W. Meyer, Jr.

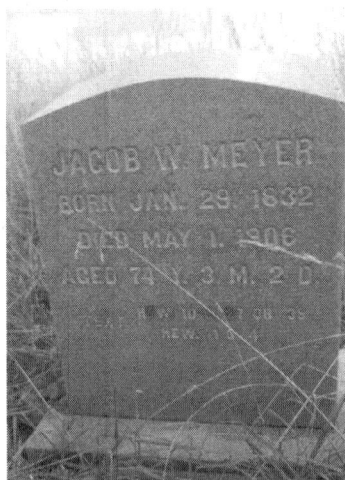

On the left is Jacob W. Meyer, Jr. He was my great-great grandfather. On the right is the tomgbstone for his father, Jacob W. Meyer. They both lived on the Meyer homestead, pictured below. This was the home for the Meyer family from 1732 until 1942 when Elmer Gibble bought the farm. The graveyard where this stone is located is on the hill on that farm.

Joseph G. Meyer

I remember my Great Grandfather, Joseph Gibble Meyer, with a long white beard, black wool pants with suspenders, a black wool vest, and a black frock coat. We called him Pop. His white shirt had long sleeves, and no collar. Today, most would confuse him with the Amish. He was very plain.

When Pop came to work at our farm, my parents would tease him about dressing so hot, even in the summertime. When he was up on the barn roof (in his 60s) painting the tin with alumacoat, he took off his frock coat and vest and left them on the ground by the ladder. When he came off the roof, the black wool went back on.

He was a patient man, as we can all testify to, when he babysat us from time to time. His concern, love and care for us could be felt.

Pop had an old Dodge car, and used to take us, his great-grandchildren, with him if he had to go on errands. We could look out the windows and practically count the blades of grass going by, because he drove at horse speed. I clearly remember watching the speedometer range from 10 to about 18 miles per hour. We all used to tease him about it as he drove, and he would just patiently smile at us kids, but he didn't speed up! Pop was born in August 1, 1882. It was a different world.

One day, at a family get together, about 1966, Pop began to talk about the changes that he had seen in his life. He was sitting in the overstuffed easy chair in the corner of the living room near the warm stove. His hands were on the arms of the chair, and he leaned forward while he talked. We all gathered around, and my father kept him talking by asking him questions. My father had recorded the broadcast that morning, so the recorder was set up, and he recorded the account. However, I believe, that many years later, that recording was lost, due to someone mistaking it and re-recording over it.

I recall his account: He was born during a time (1882) when farming was simple, small scale, totally horse driven, and field and barn work was mostly hand labor. In his community, everyone farmed. Some families only had a few acres, but that gave enough land for a big garden, some fruit trees, and room for a horse, cow, and chickens. Even in the villages, almost every house had a small barn behind the house near the alley, for the livestock. If you didn't own your own horse, you had to borrow one when you needed to travel, or you paid someone else to take you.

He saw the invention of the car, and how cars changed how people viewed the world. It seemed so much closer between towns and cities. Good roads were built, and soon people would take a day trip to places that he had never dreamed of seeing. He told how trucks revolutionized hauling freight and commerce. He lamented how local stores were all going under, because it was so easy to drive to a big store. The local villages used to have several small stores that sold everything from eggs to nuts and bolts. Those were all closing in the 1960s, as everyone could take a car and drive 20 miles to a bigger, fancier, air conditioned store. He talked about how tractors revolutionized farming. Farmers farmed more land, with less labor. Hired hands were becoming a thing of the past.

Although he saw benefits of the modernization, he also saw the price that the families and towns were paying. He saw electricity come into farms and homes.

He saw tenant houses being destroyed so famers could save on county, township and school taxes, leaving tenant families homeless. He saw small private local school houses disappear and huge consolidated school districts form under state control.

Pop saw airplanes invented, airlines form, and saw the reports of men in space. He never flew on a plane. He saw radio invented, then every home had a radio. He told how they could listen to a Chicago station, and listen to their weather for the day, and knew that would probably be their weather for tomorrow. Then, he saw televisions become available, and then commo. And, finally, he saw his first color TV. He enjoyed Hee Haw, but had little time for soap operas or dramatic shows.

He talked about how the one constant thing in his life was his faith. He was Deacon in the Church of the Brethren, read his bible every day, and was faithful in attendance. Although my Grandparents rarely went to church in the 1960s, he consistently attended. He worried that the church was changing too.

My father often talked about how he went to church withPop, his grandfather, and sat with him on the Deacon bench in the front of the church. My father got his passion for the Bible and sincere worship from Pop. He also got his passion for farming from Pop.

In the local congregation of the Church of the Brethren, there were five churches. Pop traveled to all of them on a regular basis, so my father became acquainted with all the members of the region.

The Meyer house

This meeting hall (above) stands about a mile south of Fredericksburg, Pa. Today, it has been renamed, and the Meyer name was removed, as most of the Meyer's have moved away. Below is a current picture of the church, renamed, "The Mt Zion Road Church of the Brethren."

These five churches are all within about 12 miles, and date to a time when horse and buggies were used for going to church. Actually, in the picture of the Ziegler church, you can see the horse sheds in the foreground.

The Fredericksburg house

Merkey house   Shubert house

The Merkey house has been bought by a Sacred Name group, the assembly that has been meeting at Frystown for many years. My brother, Jacob, is part of that congregation. The Schubert house has been bought and used by the Mennonites for many years.

Ziegler meetinghouse, about 1920

The Ziegler house was the closest house to my grandparents farm, and this is the one that they attended most of the time. After we came into the Sacred Names, I attended Summer Bible School here in the summer of 1962. After that, we separated ourselves more from the churches, and did not attend services or Bible Schools with them again.

Many decades after Pop died, an elderly neighbor stopped by my house and watched me training a young colt, and he commented that I definitely got that skill from Pop, because he was a renowned horse trainer in the area. That was the first time I realized his skill with horses, and began to remember the stories I heard from childhood that formed my passion for horses.

Pop died on April 5, 1969.

Jacob J. Meyer

My Grandfather, Jacob J. Meyer, was a quiet man, a farmer all his life. He was a herdsman. He called himself a herdsman. What that meant to him, was that he studied livestock all his life. He bred, raised and trained Percheron Horses. He had a dairy herd. At one time he was producing Golden Guernsey milk. He found, however, that the rich yellow color produced by the Guernsey to produce rich looking creamy colored milk, also tainted the meat with a yellow color, and that made the cows and steers hard to sell for meat.

During the depression, Pop, his father, struggled as everyone did. My grandfather and grandmother set up housekeeping on his farm, and helped Pop. Finally, when the war hit, and things got worse, they sold the farm, and they all moved to the Masonic Home at Elizabethtown.

During the Second World War, he took a job working as assistant herdsman for the Masonic Home in Elizabethtown. They had Ayrshire cows, and bulls. He learned a lot about commercial dairying there, from the head herdsman, who was from Germany.

My Grandmother cooked and cared for one of the Boy's homes. Pop worked with them as a caretaker. They all supervised the house of boys, and all three adults got paid monthly salaries. They raised their own food in the garden and lived cheaply. They banked all their wages, and added that to the money they had from selling the small farm. After the war, they took their savings, and bought a farm near Rherersburg, PA .

He started to raise Ayrshires, and had a few Jerseys over the years, but as the years went by, the milk market forced him to produce milk in high volume, not high quality taste, so he replaced the Ayrshires with Holsteins.

Jacob Owen Meyer

My grandmother, Mary, told us how my father was a blond, curly headed boy, who often stood on the kitchen chairs when he was three or four, and made believe that he was a preacher. Because his father's name was also Jacob, he was called by his middle name, Owen until he left the farm. After that, his parents still called him Owen throughout their lives.

My father's first role model was Pop, his grandfather. Next to Pop, his role models were the preachers who guided the congregation. At home the family spoke Pa Dutch, and the services were spoken in Pa Dutch, but the Bible was read in High German.

She also talked about how hard my father worked. Everyone in the family worked hard on the farm. The water had to be pumped by hand. The animals had to be cared for, fed, milked, horses harnessed, crops planted, cultivated, harvested. Wood had to be cut, hauled, split, and taken into the house every day. Equipment had to be repaired, fences mended, snow plowed, milk hauled, stove ash taken out, gardens planted, vegetables cleaned and canned, animals had to be butchered, and meat smoked and salted.

Life was hard, but without question, the whole family loved it. My father always wanted to farm. He often said that working on the farm kept him grounded. I think that when he was working with livestock, milking cows, feeding calves, and farming with horses, he was more calm, and at peace.

When my father left the farm I was just over a year old. He got a job caring for livestock so he could live in the farmhouse on that farm near Wintersville. He moved from there to another farm closer to Bernville. He cared for the livestock in the morning and evening, and worked on construction. The company he worked for communicated entirely in Pa Dutch.

He began his career by driving a dump truck, and then was assigned an early tractor-trailer. Most of the trips at that time were hauling sand from the coast of Delaware with a dump trailer. They were running Ford F8 tractors, with gas engines. It was common for a driver to come back to the shop in the evening with an engine crank hammering, and the mechanics would pull the engine, put in a new one, and the truck would be ready for the driver again in the morning.

Soon diesel trucks were on the road, and my father began to drive over the road. Although he hauled freight all over the eastern US for over 12 years, he constantly talked of farming. He would go to his parents place on his days off, and help them, because he missed farming.

He went from construction work in 1955 to hauling milk for Centerport Dairy. Then starting in 1958, he drove for Peter's Brothers of Lenhartsville, hauling livestock. Then he got a better offer from Gotwals Brothers. He drove for the Derstines, and drove for a few others over the years, and ended his driving career by hauling poultry for Grimes and Hower of Fredericksburg. He took that job at lower pay in the late 60s, so he could support the family, and be home every day, while the Assembly was growing.

Over the years, people disparaged him by labeling him as a "truck driver." Yes, he was. It provided a living, but it also gave him time to read and study. When he packed his overnight case, he always put his bible and two or three other books in there to study on layovers and rest times.

Our family

My first memories were of a typical middle class suburban family. My mother was a stay-at-home mom, caring for us, and doing housekeeping. Most women at that time did not work outside of the home. We were on the upward climb.

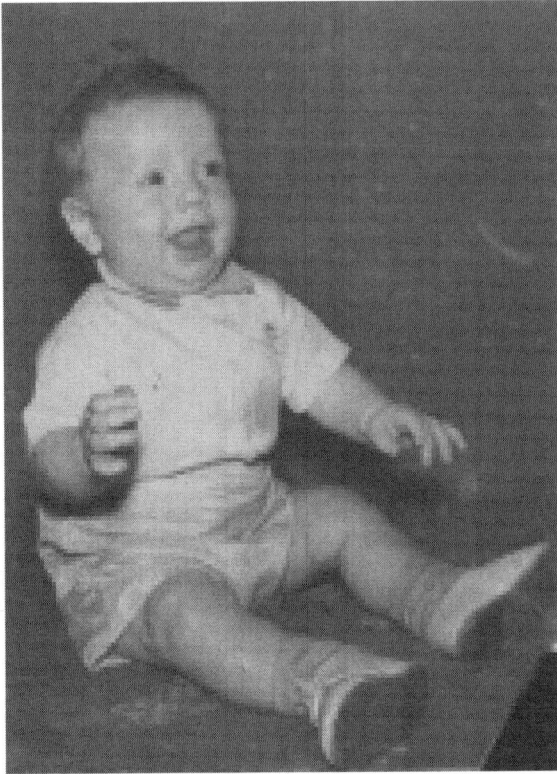

This is the author, Joseph G. Meyer about a year old. Even then I had more hair than I do today!

In 1959, we all rode to a big car lot near Philadelphia in our Rambler station wagon, and my parents traded that in on a brand new 1959 Ford Fairlane 500. They got all the options... chrome, fender skirts, dual rear antennas, and the AM/FM radio. But, that car had no air conditioning. After discussion at the car lot, about how the kids may ruin the seats, it was decided to put clear plastic slip covers on the seats. They were installed by Ford, and made the seats slippery, hot and sticky in the summer, and stiff and cold in the winter. But, the seats stayed clean.

Not only did they buy a new car, they had bought a new house in Shoemakersville. By today's standard, it was a tiny house, but was pretty typical for 1958. It had a basement, but the living area was only about 900 sq ft. We all fit in there, but three of us shared one room, so we had bunkbeds!

My parents also bought a new Compton's Encyclopedia. I loved that set of books, and spent many hours studying the pictures, and especially the color overlays of the human body systems. They bought new furniture, new pots and pans, and they socialized with other young couples in the church.

I had my fifth birthday in that house, and got a pair of black cowboy boots for my birthday present. I loved them and wore them out.

Moving to the farm, 1960

But, my father wanted to farm. In 1960, he came across a small farm property on the north side of the Reading Reservoir, Lake Ontellaunee, and my parents bought that little farm. With the cash flow from driving truck supporting the family, he figured that he could farm on the weekends, and build his assets if we all worked together. Plus, we could raise our own meat, milk, and eggs, and have a big garden to save on food.

He bought an Allis Chalmers model C tractor. Most of his implements were horse-drawn because he loved working with horses. He got two work horses, Bob and Bill, and their harness, from a friend near Bernville, John Fox. That was the team that I learned to work and drive over the next three years. He filled the barn with heifers, cows, chickens, and pigs.

My father was only home on the weekends, running two trips to Chicago or St Louis each week. He stopped by usually on Wednesday between trips. That left the daily chores on the farm to my mother and the kids. My sister Mary helped sometimes, but usually she kept track of the littlest children in the house.

Every day, I helped my mother feed the livestock, and take out manure. She got me a little three gallon bucket to help haul water from the faucet to water the livestock. We had running water in the barn, but no plastic or rubber hoses. Remember, plastic was not yet common on the farm, and rubber products were inferior and didn't last. My little bucket was galvanized tin, and the big buckets were the same. These buckets were guarded and protected because they cost so much and could be destroyed quickly by a steer or a horse if they stepped in it.

It was a hard life for my mother. Compared to most young women today, she willingly worked long hours on the farm, in the house, and raised the children through it all. Multi-tasking? That was our way of life. When we moved there, There were four children: Mary (b 1953), me (b. 1954), Jake (b. 1956), and Daniel (b. 1959).

Every year we raised the calves and as the steers grew, they were destined for butchering. We raised pigs, and I was amazed at how quickly they grew. One night, it was raining and freezing, and my mother had me mix up the feed slop for the pigs, while she milked the cows. The pig pen was across the road. The feed was in two five gallon buckets, not quite full.

I could not carry them, so my mother had to. She would take a bucket in each hand, and go out the side door of the barn through the feed alley in front of the horses, and out across the road. She didn't realize on that night that the cold rain had frozen on the blacktop, and when she was out on the road, her feet flew out from underneath her, and she fell hard on her back. The pig slop flew all over her, and made a huge puddle that froze on the street.

For the rest of her life, she struggled with back pain, certainly not improved by having six more children! She went into the house to change, limping as she went, and I stayed and mixed two more buckets of slop feed, and I carried them through the barn one at a time, and then skated them across the road one at a time to finish the feeding. I was six years old, but the hogs needed to be fed.

Every winter, usually in February, we butchered. A large wooden tripod was set up in the barn yard. A fire was built and the butcher furnace was put around it. My Great grandfather, Pop, brought most of the equipment to butcher, and he helped. My dad had been butchering all his life, so he ran the show. All the men in the family had butchered all their lives, so the butchering of the animals was like a production line. My other Grandfather, Grandpa Foreman was available in the evening, so he came and helped in the evening. His dad was a butcher, and he had the best scrapple recipe I ever tasted.

My dad was quite a good shot, and I never saw him have to take a second shot to put down the steer or pig. It was expected in our family that you only took one shot. We didn't waste bullets, or cause the animal undue pain.

The lard was cooked to boiling, and the cracklins were skimmed off and put in chip cans, that were then stored in the attic. I used to sneak up there and snack on the cracklins when no one was around. The hams and bacons were smoked, and they were stored in the root cellar.

Walking down into the root cellar was always an adventure for me. It was dark, close, damp, and smelled like the wet earth. The only light came down the narrow stone stairway. There, in the dim light, it was my job every week to take salt from the bucket and rub the hams and bacons hard, to keep the mold from growing. I remember how cold and gritty that felt. They had to be turned and rubbed on the bottom too.

Saluting the Flag

Our farm had two dwellings on it. The main farm house, and right next to it connected by a short sidewalk, was a small tenant house. When we first moved there, a family lived there who were Jehovah's Witnesses. They had a little girl about two years older than me. As we played, we would of course talk as kids will do. One day she mentioned that she did not salute the flag, because we were not supposed to worship anything here on earth. We should only worship Jehovah, so we should not salute the flag.

That made sense to me, so when I started school that fall, I told the teacher that I did not salute the flag, and she had me go out into the hallway while the rest of the class saluted the flag. Thus began my life as a renegade. Throughout my school years, as we became more and more strict, I would think back to this, my first decision to worship as I believed. This early decision by me, on my own, helped me to accept all other withdrawals from organized religion and reactions to popular worship.

Of course, in later years, I would ask myself if I would have been a spiritual person on my own, outside of my parent's faith. This small step in first grade convinced me that I would have always striven for truth and tried to obey what I found.

A year later, when my parents decided that we should not salute the flag, I told them that I had never saluted the flag. I remember how stunned they were and how they looked at each other in shock.

Church Services

During the late 50s, evangelists such as Billy Graham, Kathryn Kuhlman, and many others followed the tradition of Billy Sunday and Aimee Semple-McPherson in holding large revivals in stadiums to stir up the dedication of the churches. My father attended a number of these before 1960. He attended Bible classes at Albright College. He and my mother took a Bible Course from the Seventh Day Adventists, and later took the Correspondence Course from Herbert Armstrong, of Pasadena, Ca. Religion and religious studies were a big part of our lives.

These studies raised the questions about the Sabbath (from the SDAs and the COG), and the clean foods. Armstrong taught the feast days too. These questions about doctrines came up during Bible study, and my parents would discuss whether we should be practicing those Old Testament laws. Within the church, those topics were not discussed at all.

Jonathan was born in 1961. My mother did the farm work up to the day he was born. Every evening, on the road, my father would call collect, for John Meyer. If my mother said he was not home, my father knew we were still waiting, and he didn't have to spend money for the call.

Then one day after my father called, my mother walked away from the phone, and her water broke. It was confusing for me, as I suddenly connected human birth to animal births, and realized she was having the baby. She called the doctor, and I helped her mop the floor. Then, she put the kids to bed, and got things ready for the birth. The doctor arrived just as Jonathan was appearing, and I watched the birth, in my parent's bedroom, under the elbow of the doctor.

During this time on the small farm, my father was a Sunday School teacher, and the series he was teaching was titled: the Acts of the Apostles. Every Saturday, my father would lay his books out on the coffee table in the living room, with his cup of coffee and his cigarettes.

Yes, he smoked, and my mother did not. She fussed at him for five years as he struggled to quit. Finally, in 1964, I can say that I saw him smoke his last cigarette. From then on, he was sympathetic to people who were addicted, but he constantly encouraged them to gain victory over their addiction as he finally did.

His favorite Bibles at that time were the **KJV**, the **ASV**, **the Moffat Bible**, and **Rotherham**. As soon as it was available locally, he also began to use the **Companion Bible** because of the extensive notes that were so informative. He used the **Strong's Concordance**. He would lay all these books out on the table, with the study outline for the weekly lesson from the Church of the Brethren, and then he would study the passage for the week in its context, reading each version, studying the language, the origins of the words, how they were translated to gain a deep knowledge of what the author of the book was trying to relate to us, the readers. During this time, his library began to grow, from one bookshelf to three, as I recall.

The Acts of the Apostles. This series of lessons was an eye opener for my father. As my father studied this series of lessons from the Church of the Brethren, and taught them in Sunday School, he kept asking us at home, "Why don't we see these acts of faith in the church today?" His questions were persistent. Where was the Holy Ghost today? Why were the gifts of the spirit so hard to find? Was the church doing something wrong?

Many of the young couples my parents socialized with were too busy forming their young families, and most really didn't want to investigate their path to salvation too deeply. Only a couple of them would discuss the topics with my father.

One person he could always discuss the Bible with was John Fox. John Fox was an enigma. He was a farmer, and a horseman, but he stuttered, and stammered continually. My father told me that his speech impediment began after he had an emotional breakdown while in College. He was always dressed in dirty coveralls. Somehow, he had gone to a theological school in his youth, and still loved to talk about the Bible, with my dad. He knew a lot, had many good ideas, and my dad respected him for it.

During this time, we attended services with a Holiness Church at Birdsboro several times. My father wanted to see a modern example of the Holy Ghost in action. Coming from the quiet and reserved Church of the Brethren, this was new to all of us. This was my first experience with seeing how some congregations would tarry for the spirit; how they would sing choruses over and over, and get louder and louder, some people were continually hollering for the spirit, until tongues and prophecies would erupt all over the church. For a six year old, it was fascinating. I watched to see who got the spirit, and learned which type of people were prone to those displays.

Trouble in the Church

In the summer of 1961, the Church of the Brethren held several picnics for the congregation. I enjoyed these tremendously, as we kids were able to run about and play with the other kids, a rare thing when raised on a farm. At the fourth of July picnic, the young adult men went down into the trees across from the church, and set off firecrackers. Some of them used the more powerful ones called cherry bombs, to blow up tin cans, and make loud booms. The older men stayed at the church, and frowned and shook their heads. When we ran to the street to see what they were doing, the women caught us and sent us back to the playground. Firecrackers and cherry bombs were not for kids to play with.

After the picnic, my parents felt a bit guilty for the church to be turning more worldly and getting involved with firecrackers and such. That type of fun was frowned upon traditionally. Even fun activities were to be justified as educational, upbuilding, or constructive. Activities that were destructive or just to create excitement were considered worldly.

In the fall of 1961, the Church had a Halloween party. This really bothered my parents, and they did not attend. The young couples wanted this kind of popular socializing, but to my parents, this was too close to witchcraft and devil worship. They believed that to celebrate Halloween was leaving the light, and following darkness. I began to hear them ask each other, "Who is in charge of this church?" When reports came back of risqué activities at the party, the questions became more fervent. It was obvious to me, that they wanted some Elder to step up, and put a stop to such activities. They wanted the Elders to control the church. They also wanted the Elders to put out those who sinned and to shun them.

This is a historical struggle in the Church of the Brethren. The Church of the Brethren really has no creed. Very briefly, to belong to the Church of the Brethren, you must accept Jesus as your lord and savior, you must strive to live an exemplary life, and you must work with the brethren to build the church. When ideas that were alien to the membership began to come into the church, someone would arise to preach against it, and the church would be full of dissent until some people left, and it calmed down again. In essence, they practiced shunning when situations got disruptive enough. But it was not a church doctrine. My parents began to believe that it was necessary for peace.

From the first debate over the proper Sabbath day in the early 1700s, the Church of the Brethren has struggled with trying to maintain the freedom of conscience of the individual, while working hard to keep the fraternal union of the brethren. They try to be inclusive of all who strive for salvation, but in practice, human nature overrules that tolerance too often, and divisions happen.

My father began to outline things he thought that the church should require. Later, this became the Statement of Doctrine that he proposed for the Assemblies of Yahweh. By creating a creed, he was already essentially leaving the basic concept of the Church of the Brethren. He retained many of their practices throughout his life, keeping the parts of their tradition he was most comfortable with. We always have sung their favorite songs, kept communion much as they did, maintained the kiss of fellowship, and many other traditions he was raised with.

Chapter 2

A Historic Visit

About November of 1961, he got a call from two friends of his from the church. They wanted to come and visit with him. They heard through the grapevine that he was seeking something, and they felt they had something to offer him. They had both left the church with their families about a year earlier, and of course, that made them suspect, but as my parents were seeking truth, they were willing to have them over for a personal visit. Mr. and Mrs Harold Schaeffer and Mr and Mrs Charles Graeff came over for the memorable visit.

I remember the night they came over. We kids had spent the day helping my mother clean the house, she cooked a nice big supper, and we cleaned up the meal before they got there. She had intended to invite them for supper, but they declined, and came over after supper. The house was warm, cheery, and smelled great from the meal when they arrived. They accepted dessert and coffee, and the adults all moved to the living room. The kids were sent to quietly play in the side room that opened into both the living room and the kitchen. I sneaked into the corner of the living room and listened in.

After some small talk, Mr Graeff dived right in and asked my father if he knew the true name of God. My father answered, "Of course, his name is Yahweh." The visitors both sat back and looked at each other with surprise. Then Mr Graeff leaned forward again, and asked, "Why don't you use it?" That made my father sit back and reflect. He and my mother looked at each other in silence for a few minutes. They could not honestly answer that question.

From that moment, they decided to change the way they viewed the Bible. They kept asking the question, "… then why don't we do it?" for each doctrinal question. Instead of justifying what they were raised to do, they asked why they should not do each commanded activity spoken about in the Bible. For the rest of the evening, the conversation toured through the clean food laws, the Sabbath, and many other practices discussed in the Bible. From then on, we never ate pork. We kept the seventh Day Sabbath, and studied the commandments of the Bible in depth.

Our Last Christmas

While we sat in the living room studying the Bible, in the family room in the corner, was a large Christmas tree. Although they talked about so many things that night, they never touched on Christmas and the other holidays. To this day, I find that ironic, as labeling everything popular and Christian as Pagan is such a Sacred Name movement tendency.

During the next weeks, as my parents studies, Christmas came and went. That was our last Christmas. I received two gift that year that I remember. My parents bought me a large red fire truck with ladders and lights all made of plastic.

I really enjoyed playing with that, as any boy would. Later that winter, I came in from the barn one morning, and the whole house stank. Mary told my mother that she could not figure out why the house smelled so bad.

I searched around, and saw that there were red stains on the heat duct in the living room. A large duct above the furnace brought the heat straight into the house. I ran down to the basement, and opened the duct door, and there on top of the furnace was a red puddle. That was all that was left of my fire truck. My brother Jake (who probably doesn't even remember this!) had been playing with my fire truck and left it on the grate while we were out in the barn, and it melted.

I scraped off as much of the plastic as I could, so it would not catch on fire when the furnace got really hot, and threw it away. That was the end of that gift.

The other gift I remember was a holster and guns. I loved western movies, and had worn boots for over a year until they wore out, so my grandmother thought I would like some play cap guns. I was so proud, wearing my guns and running around playing cowboy, using up the caps scaring people. That made my grandparents laugh. After they left, my mother took the guns away and hid them. She did not think that guns were appropriate for children to play with.

Making Big Changes in Our Lives

This created a problem with the pigs in the pigpen across the road from the barn. They were slated to be butchered in February, and my mother and father decided to continue with the butchering, and to sell the meat after it was cured. Well, butcher day came and went.

I was in first grade at this time, and I was so proud to take a bull's eyeball to school for show and tell. My grandfather Foreman was behind that fiasco. If you knew him, you would understand. He had also told me that the way to get your teacher to like you, was to spit on her shoe the first day of school. I suspected that was a joke, thank goodness.

But, I couldn't see what was wrong with taking a cool item like an eyeball for show and tell. So, my Grandfather dug it out of the skull, and I put it into a quart Mason jar with water, and took it to school the next day. My teacher was appalled when she saw the eyeball floating in water. I was so proud, no one else had ever brought an eyeball to class before. She was not impressed and it got sent home with me again that night.

The hams and bacons were sent to the Bashore's to put in the smoke house. Several weeks later, my dad got a call from them, apologizing because the smokehouse had burned down, and all the hams and bacons were burnt and ruined. When my dad said that was ok, they were stunned, because that meat was worth a lot of money. They did not yet know that we had stopped eating pork, and my parents viewed this as a sign that we should not even profit from raising pork. My father gave the hams to some friends who were willing to cut off the burnt parts and salvage what they could.

During this time, my parents often went to Hamburg for services on the Sabbath at Minnie Boltz's house. Her husband was not a believer, but we met in their home. Typically, there were about a dozen people meeting there.

We rode on a school bus every day to attend the Mulltown Elementary School. This school had three classrooms for six grades. Each teacher taught two grades. On that bus the meanest, oldest boy was always tormenting us. One morning he told me that he didn't want me sitting near him, because my dad was a killer. I was shocked, not knowing what he was talking about. We shouted back and forth a bit, until the bus driver told us to shut up. I clammed up about it on the bus, and during school, but I fretted about it all day. When I got home that night, I told my mother what had happened and asked her what he was talking about.

She told me of the accident that my father had just had the night before out in the Midwest, when a man, changing his car tire close by the road, had fallen onto the road, and was killed by the truck my father was driving. It had been on the TV news, but we did not have a TV at that time. They had even jailed my father, so he could not leave the state. Thankfully, the coroner quickly found that the man actually died of a heart attack before he fell onto the road, and my father was released with no charges. However, that was a sobering time for my father. When he had stopped the truck and ran back to help the family, the man's little boy ran to him, pummelling him with his fists, and crying, "You killed my daddy." My father held him while he cried, and that memory and the cries of that boy never left my father.

That winter and spring, I helped my father taking out the manure with a manure sled and the horses. It took many days to take out the manure pile in the barnyard from the winter livestock waste. That was the job we did when he taught me to drive the team of horses. I learned the feeling of the horses in my hand, how to communicate with them through the heavy leather lines, and to feel their response to each command. I learned to work in partnership with the horse, and have never lost that wonderful feeling.

In the spring of 1962, my father used the tractor to plow and work the ground, and planted the corn with the horses. Then he cultivated the corn and I watched it grow each week. However, during the early summer, a terrible hail storm came and destroyed the entire crop. It was cut down to the ground, and all that work was gone. It was too late to plant more corn, and my parents faced another huge loss. First, they lost the pork meat from the seasons before, and now they had no corn coming in for the winter. They knew that they could not survive a year without corn, and the loss ended my father's dream of farming.

Moving to Bethel

At this time, every word and event were evaluated from the position of language, and meanings were attributed to every event. With their studies of the patriarchs, they saw that the names of the locations also told a story. This is outlined in the Companion Bible, in Appendix 50.

Names, numbers, and types became important. For example, when they had to decide where to move, my Grandparents offered to help them. This meant we were moving to Bethel. What does Bethel mean? The House of El. Therefore, this was a good move. Later, when they moved to Job's Corner's, that was a time of testing and proving if they would be faithful. Then they moved to Wilder, Idaho. That was a suspicious name, and explained why it was not peaceful. Turner, Oregon, showed a change of direction, and then we moved back to Bethel.

This approach to living is very familiar to all in the Sacred Name Movement. Everything becomes spiritualized. Later in life, when I was friends with a person who studied Psychology, our discussion of this topic opened his eyes to what he labeled as the "emotional and the insecure" aspects of religion.

My parents made plans to discontinue farming and to sell the farm. They traded the heifers to a man that sold mobile homes, and used that money as down payment for a 12 x 60 mobile home with three bedrooms. I remember that it was a Rembrandt brand, blue and white in color. It was set up on the edge of my Grandfather Foreman's garden area, and we ran water pipe from his house and installed a septic tank.

When we moved, my father loaded all the farm equipment in the old horse drawn Gruber hay flat wagon and pulled that by tractor from Leesport to Bethel. I rode on the fender of the tractor. That was a long trip!

We lived there at my grandparent's farm for about a year. During that time, my father farmed my grandfather's land (about 12 acres) and that of Ann Ranck, at that time about 40 acres. I attended the end of second grade (about 6 weeks) and all of third grade at Bethel Elementary School, and rode Harold Bashore's bus every day.

Religion and School

By this time, we also had to make changes in school. First of all was the issue of saluting the flag. Although I never saluted the flag in my entire school career, I know that some of my siblings decided not to be so different, and they never told their teacher, so they would not have to go to the hallway.

My parents never checked on whether or not we actually practiced what we talked about at home. Freedom of conscience and free will were important to my parents. If they had learned about it, I know they would not have intervened. When we stopped eating pork, my one brother said that he loved pork chops, and that when he got old he would eat pork chops. My parents laughed about that for years, knowing that someday, he would have to make that decision as an adult.

I don't think he ever went out and bought pork chops. As an adult he chose to continue his observance of the clean food laws. Other siblings of mine stopped observing the food laws as soon as they left the house.

Lunches were the daily reminder that we were different. Every week we got the school menu and which day we packed lunches depended on which days they had pork. We usually packed lunch for two reasons: the money, and the clean foods. I ate a lot of cheese and bologna sandwiches and peanut butter and jelly sandwiches. Later on, the free lunch program came in, and our income was so low, with so many kids, that we got free lunches.

In later years, I always ate lunch in the cafeteria, and I learned that I could trade a hot dog for vegetables any day. I learned to like vegetables. When others saw the trade, if they hated carrots or peas, they would pass them down, so sometimes I got a big plate of vegetables.

All of this made us different.

Then, the classes also had to be considered. In art class, every holiday was remembered with some type of project we had to make. Usually, with every holiday, there is a religious and a secular interpretation. I did a lot of snowman pictures, bunnies and little chicks.

In music class, it was even worse. We had a little concert in school every holiday. For weeks before that concert, we would be singing songs about the holiday. Some of them were overtly religious, and were full of false doctrines. Some of them were neutral. Some of them were secular. I always told my music teacher about not observing the holidays, so I was excluded. Sometimes, I had to go and sit in the office while they had music class. Sometimes the teacher would move my desk to the hallway for music class. Again, I was different.

In third grade, with all the commotion leading up to the concert, my teacher forgot that I should be excluded, and I could not get her attention. So, with all the other kids, I marched onto the stage, wearing my green wool winter coat and red scarf, and sang 'Frosty the Snowman" with everyone else, and made believe while they sang "Silent Night."

Chapter 3

Sacred Name Services

Each Sabbath, we continued going to services at Minnie Boltz's home in Hamburg. (Her son-in law, Nevin Groff and her daughter Mary were members of the Assembly of Yahweh in later years.) We were the only family that brought children to services, and although we children were very good during services, after services they always had a meal together and then a Bible study. The day got long, and we got restless. One day, while they were getting the food set out for lunch, we went out in the yard to play off some energy, and discovered that it sounded cool to jump on her steel basement doors. It really made a racket, and we were stopped immediately, and after that we were never taken there again. My parents would arrange for a baby sitter to watch us at home. Often, it was my aunt Linda, my mother's youngest sister. We liked having her as a baby sitter, because she was such a kind and gentle girl.

As other families learned about the Bible Studies and worship, the Boltz'es house got crowded. The services were more or less moderated by Pastor Crowell at that time. He found a little vacant church that he either bought or rented, and services were moved there. I don't know where that was, although it was quite a drive. I recently drove past a little brick church near York, on Crowell Road, that looked like that little church, and I wonder if that is where we attended.

Dissent began to surface in the congregation, and I often heard my parents discuss it on the way home. My parents thought that there was too much hesitation in keeping some of the commandments, and that the messages were too weak. We began to stay at home for Sabbath Services and just worship as a family. I remember after we missed a couple of services, that Pastor Crowell drove to our house and had a discussion about it, and they parted ways amicably.

During this time, my parents had a visit from a Jehovah Witness family, and we began to have Bible Studies with them. For decades after this, we were on the mailing list for the **Watchtower** and **Awake** magazines. All of us children read anything that came in the mail, so we learned a lot of religious doctrines from the magazines our parents received. The studies with the Jehovah's Witnesses stopped when my father was gone one week, and during the study, the lady insisted that we read the material as written.

I could not bring myself to say God or Lord, and she insisted and demanded that I read those names. I just could not utter them, and she got rough about it. My mother stopped the study, and asked them to leave, and that ended the studies with the Jehovah' s Witnesses. However, their book, **Paradise Lost,** was always a favorite of mine.

My parents continued to study, and to receive magazines from churches and pastors from all over the world. They wrote letters to other believers, and some were published in various Sacred Name magazines. Almost every month, **The Kingdom Herald**, **The Faith**, the **Mt Zion Reporter**, **The Plain Truth**, and others would arrive in the mail. Through those magazines, my parents began to meet others of like mind.

We traveled to Philadelphia (Morton) and had services with Al and Doris Francis, Ruth Fink and Mrs. Schultz. At this time, The Francis's were publishing **the Faith** magazine. We met Elder Ziegler from Cheltenham Ave in Philadelphia. He was a tall, spare man, with a quick smile. He was an avid British Israelite believer, and every sermon he taught was about the stone of scone, the possibility that the royal family had the blood of Yahshua's family in it, and much about the old Irish and British religions being derived from the Israelite faith of the time of David and Solomon.

We also met Paul Penn, and he and my father formed a strong friendship. Paul offered to teach my father Hebrew, and they began lessons whenever we visited Philadelphia. Paul Penn probably knew every librarian in Philadelphia! Every visit, he would take us to a library, and show my father through the stacks, talking about which books were the best for Hebrew studies.

My father would borrow books from him, and read them on the road during the week. He was especially fond of Dropsie College (Dropsie College for Hebrew and Cognate Learning). He was close friends with the librarian there. When my father would go into the library with Paul, my mother would take the children for a walk in the park. I would shadow my father and Paul, and hang out in the library with them and try to follow their discussions about the Holocaust, Jewish history, the Talmud, and the Mishnah.

For many years, my father subscribed to the **Jewish Quarterly Review**, published by Dropsie College. In 1993, they had a terrible fire in the library, and many rare single copy books were destroyed and lost forever.

Paul Penn introduced us to Jewish dietary foods such as Borscht, Gefilte Fish, and my favorite: Blintzes. There was a small Jewish restaurant named the Blintze.

One afternoon, the waiter there set down a hot cup of coffee in front of my dad, and Daniel (four at the time) was the only one who saw him set it down. Daniel picked it up and took a burning hot sip and proceeded to scream bloody murder. The waiter felt so badly he gave us all a treat. Paul Penn was fond of drinking selzer water, and to this day, when I see seltzer water in the store, I think of him. I will occasionally buy some for the memories, but can't get any of my kids to drink it!

We traveled to New Jersey, and at Irvington, attended services with A.B. Traina. There we met Etta Glenn and many others. Typically on a weekly Sabbath there were only a dozen or so people attending his services. But that was typical of the Sacred Name Movement. His girls had already left home by the time we were attending, so I don't think I ever met them. During his sermons, Elder Traina showed his studious side. He quoted from reference books, dictionaries, Bible Versions, and of course peppered the sermon with Bible verses to build a case for his doctrines, and to teach the congregation. He used logic and proofs, in a manner much like my father did.

He had a table flanked by two benches, and he would do his Bible studies there. I remember being a shadow one time, and he asked me to come and sit by him. During that study, he and my father got on the subject of the Day of Atonement, and he got really heated. That is putting it mildly. He was Italian, and he put all his emotion into his discussions! It scared me, sitting beside him with all the shouting, when our family was so reserved. That subject never was resolved between them. He felt that Yahshua was our atonement, and we should not keep the Old Testament day. He felt we should rejoice always, not fast on that day.

He had other doctrines that he was rather alone on. He believed in spirit beings mating with human women in Genesis 6, for one. It seems that any time we visited there, we would hear someone get on these subjects, and the arguments would boil on and on.

During this whole time, my father was driving truck to make a living, and he was still wanting to farm. On weekends, we would occasionally go to Tioga County to my grandfather's cabin, and my parents would look around at farms with the idea that they just wanted to move to a wilderness area to raise their family away from the increasing corruption of the world, and to study the Bible in peace. As my father later described it, he had become very disillusioned with the lack of progress and the lack of any viable program moving the Sacred Name Movement toward any goal. He didn't see any push to get the message out to the world.

Even though there were magazines published all over the US, they all pushed different ideas. Too often, visits from pastors looked like they were just traveling to steal members from each other. Other groups, my father said, sat around and sang to each other. It sounds harsh, but does describe what he saw.

My parents found a farm in Tioga County, at Job's Corner, just up the hill from the Jennings's Pony Farm. Job's Corners was just north of Roseville, and only about five miles from the New York state line. This farm had a unique feature, the land was all in soil bank, and the government paid the owner to mow the hay, and not to plant crops. This worked well with my father driving truck, and provided the cash flow he needed to buy it. We moved there in the summer of 1963.

Paul and Aggie Kwiatkowski

During this time, our most regular worship away from home was with the Kwiatkowski's. Paul and Agnes were a Polish couple from Shamokin. About once a month, we would travel to Shamokin and meet with four or five friends of theirs for services. They loved to hear children sing, and every Sabbath that we were there, we children had to sing three of four songs. Paul's favorite song was, "A Child of the King." We sang that every time.

They were retired, and spent their time as evangelists, traveling and meeting with Sacred Name Believers around the U.S. They arrived at our home one time driving a VW minibus, all fitted out as a camper. That was before the days of the RV, and it was quite a novelty. Paul was very dogmatic that they would not stay at any one place over three days. He used to say that visitors were just like a fish, after three days, you better get rid of it, or it would begin to stink.

After services on the Sabbath, we were given a late lunch by Aggie every week. She loved cooking and feeding those who came for services. After lunch, we weren't allowed to leave. Paul and Aggie were very strict about keeping the Sabbath. They could justify driving to services on Sabbath morning, but felt strongly that the Sabbath was not over until 6 pm. So, we had to wait until 6 pm to leave. We would sit and nap, or take walks, but we had to wait.

My parents were not that restrictive about driving on the Sabbath, and we kept the Sabbath from Sundown to Sundown. Paul and Aggie and my parents had numerous discussions about the 6 pm Sabbath. They felt it was just too confusing to follow sundown, since with cloudy or stormy weather or if you were in town, as they were, you couldn't see the sun. So, they felt strongly we should just set a time, and follow that. They were pretty strict about clean foods. I recall one time that they bought a box of doughnuts for lunch, and during lunch someone noticed that the box listed lard as an ingredient. Aggie threw it right out.

On Passover, Aggie and Paul would put the leaven outside in a cooler. After the days of Unleavened Bread, they would bring it back in. My parents disagreed, saying that you should not bring sin back after a cleansing. In later years, we began to give the leavened items to poor families in our area. These minor disagreements on practice of the commandments happened constantly in the Sacred Name Movement, and continue to this day.

My parents wanted all practice to be standardized. I have come to see the need for tolerance, giving each person a chance to study, to learn, to practice according to their conscience. We are not all at the same place on our spiritual journey, and we all face different circumstances. Compassion and tolerance should rule. At that time, my parents were getting more and more strict, and taking a more literal interpretation for every doctrine. This fueled their disillusionment with the Sacred Name Groups.

During the summer, my parents became convinced that they needed to be re-baptised into the name of Yahshua. They took that verse literally, and decided that their prior baptism had been incorrect, and they needed to be baptized in the Sacred Name for salvation. The discussed for some time what they should do. They were afraid that if they were baptized too closely to any organized group, that their baptism would be tied to that group, with whatever doctrines they taught, and with whatever error the held. They did not want to go through repeated baptisms, but felt that who did the baptism was important.

Ruth Fink of Morton, PA, was especially insistent that they should come to Morton to be immersed. My father did not disagree with the location, but he wanted Paul Kwiatkowski to do the actual baptism. So, during the summer, we traveled to Morton, and my parents were immersed into the Sacred Name, by Paul Kwiatkowski.

On one of our trips to Shamokin, my father had on the radio, and we heard a really catchy song, "I Want to Hold Your Hand." I heard my parents singing along with it, and only later learned that it was sung by the group called the "Beatles." That memory is fresh and strong, and includes looking out the window and seeing a Gulf gas station that advertised gas at 32.9 cents a gallon. We all miss those days!

In the late 1960s, about 1967, Paul had a stroke, and was confined to bed as a total invalid. Aggie spent her last years caring for him with total devotion.

Life on the farm at Job's Corner

That summer, Rachel was born in August. The doctor came to the house, driving a black Corvette. For him, there were no speed limits. All the police knew that he did home deliveries, and he never got stopped for speeding. When my mother was shocked how fast he got there from Mansfield, he laughed and said he was doing over 120 mph on the straight stretches. I think he loved his job.

Before I move on, I have to share a story about our studies with the Seventh Day Adventists. In the area was a Seventh Day Adventist who had a real evangelizing spirit. He heard about how my father was a Bible student and was seeking truth. Somehow, they got together, and we met with him for several weeks. I remember that when we drove to his house, either he or the neighbor had a beautiful herd of pure white, Charolais cattle in the field. Ever since that time, I have loved seeing Charolais cattle.

Charolais cattle grazing.

Well, we met with him for several weeks, and it settled into him coming to our house every Friday night for a Bible study. After we covered all the common doctrines of interest, he began to push the writings of Ellen G. White strongly. My father tried over and over to tell him that we were not interested in studying the writings of Ellen G. White. He would not listen, so then my father tried to discontinue the Bible studies.

He would not stop showing up every Friday evening. Finally, my parents got tired of it and made sure we went away from home every Friday evening. One Friday, however, we had no real place to go, so we turned all the lights off, and kept quiet while he knocked loudly on the door, and called out for my mother and father to see if we were home. Finally, he left, and got the idea that we really did not want to study with him anymore.

Piano Lessons on The Sabbath

When school began, the music teacher also taught lessons for the children. I went to her and told her that I really wanted to learn the piano, could she teach me? We talked, and she said she would try to set that up with the school. I knew that some of the children had trumpet, violin, and flute lessons at recess, and I greatly anticipated learning piano at recess. Giving up a recess would have been well worth getting lessons.

Well, the next week, she handed the class a sheet advertising the piano lessons. She was going to give piano lessons on Saturday mornings. My heart sank, but I went home and tried my best to have my parents agree to let me take piano lessons with her for free on Saturday morning. They would not bend. The Sabbath was for worship, not taking piano lessons. This was the first time I began to question how people interpreted the Bible. I could not understand why I could not take lessons, to play piano, when I saw people playing piano at services.

My parents promised me that I could get piano lessons later. It never happened, and I never learned how to play piano. Later on, I did learn to play a little guitar, violin, and I was a tuba player in the High School Band.

The Feasts

In 1963, there was no standard for feast keeping. Most of the Sacred Name families kept Passover. Some kept the Days of Unleavened Bread. A few kept Pentecost. Almost none kept the Feast of Trumpets or Atonement. Some kept the Feast of Tabernacles, but almost none lived in a temporary dwelling during the Feast of Tabernacles.

This was the first year that my parents became convinced that we should all fast on the Day of Atonement. The day was a serious, holy day, so no work was done. From sundown to sundown, we fasted. This was a total fast, no food or water. They decided that we should all sleep late, so that we would not get so hungry. Well, we did get up rather early, that being our habit, and while my father was studying the Bible, we were sent out to take a walk. We casually walked up the hill... and right past the orchard. It didn't take any planning for us kids to sneak into the orchard, and begin to pick up apples and pears, and have an impromptu lunch.

Of course, one of the youngest tattled on us, and we were lectured on the need to be obedient to the

Word, even if adults were not watching. The youngest children were fed crackers or ate cereal, and had water to drink, but no meals were cooked.

My mother had become convinced that we needed to keep all the feasts strictly. My father agreed, but had to make a living, so during that feast of Tabernacles in 1963, he worked. When he came home, he drove in the driveway, walked into the house at night, and couldn't find us. For a minute, he thought my mother had left him and taken the kids! But he came looking, and found us camping in the summer house, sleeping on the floor on mattresses.

He came into the dark summer house, and I remember their quick discussion about keeping the feast. She expressed her concern that we keep the feast right, and my father listened. Then he took off his shoes, climbed into the bed, and said, "Then, from now on, we keep it right." And, from that day on, we kept the Feast of Tabernacles outside of our home, in a temporary dwelling. That was also the last feast that my father kept while working a job during the feast.

As the year passed on the farm in Tioga County, my parents began to feel guilty about hiding away from the world while the message of salvation was neglected. We had a comfortable life. We had a big garden, and canned most of our food. We had an orchard behind the house for fruit. We had pastures and a big barn, and were planning on getting livestock. We had chickens for eggs. It was a great place for kids to get out and run and play. We made friends with the Jennings's, and my father bought us a pony.

About once a month, we traveled long miles to meet with other believers as described above. Constantly, questions were asked, by everyone we met with: "What can we do to proclaim this message of truth?" Many ideas were put forward, but no one acted on them. During this time, my parents saw a notice in the **Sacred Name Herald** from Earl Boyd, asking for help in his print shop, and with his ministry. The more they talked about it, the more convinced they became that they should move to Idaho and help put forward the truth they believed in.

Chapter 4

Moving to Idaho

Earl Boyd offered the use of his tenant house in exchange for help. He promised that there was employment in the area. He talked of setting up an agricultural community on some land he had in upstate Idaho in the future. It sounded promising, and my parents became eager to help proclaim truth.

Very quickly, they made plans to move to Idaho. In the early spring, they put a hitch on the 1959 Ford sedan, loaded up a U-Haul trailer, with all their most important personal household possessions, books, and clothing, and we left Tioga County. The day we left, they had a lady from a used furniture shop come out, and she agreed to take all the furniture and household goods that didn't fit in the trailer. She gave them $100 for all of it. My parents were upset, because a lot of the furniture was really nice and nearly new. But, they made the deal because they were committed to going to Idaho to help in the ministry.

As we stood by the car, ready to leave, the skies grew dark, and we heard a blood chilling sound. In the heavens above us there was a loud argument. Even today, the hair on my arms stands on end remembering it. It was a language we could not understand, but the sound was that of an argument rolling across the heavens. From side to side, horizon to horizon, we could hear the heavenly fight going on. It was not thunder, it was voices, shrill and insistent. It was if one party wanted us to go, and one wanted us to stay.

We were frozen is place listening to it, and not knowing what was going to happen. Gradually, it subsided, the earth grew quiet, the birds began to sing again, and the sun came out. With deep, shaking breaths, my parents discussed what had just happened. They still felt strongly that this was Yahweh's will, so we got in the car, and left.

My uncle, Landis, married to my dad's sister, Mildred, came up with his dump truck and loaded all the tools and farm equipment, and took the pony. He put the pony in the back of the dump truck and drove three hours. I wish I could have seen that! He later told me that it was cute; occasionally the pony would raise his head and look out, and startle the cars following the truck.

That trip was a big event for us. We travelled across the US pulling a U-Haul, leaving everyone and everything behind. Starting a new life is invigorating at the time, I guess. We stopped occasionally as we drove at historic sites. One site we stopped at was near the Platte River of Nebraska. There we saw the deep grooves cut into the rocks by the wagons on the Oregon Trail.

We stopped at Fort Bridger, in Wyoming. We also stopped in Laramie for the Sabbath, stayed in a motel, and spent the day at the museum. When we left there, we drove uphill for almost a day, as we climbed the Rockies. What an experience that was! My father was mostly concerned for that poor car, as it was hauling a heavy load.

We arrived at Earl Boyd's, and saw the tenant house. It was tiny. It had one bedroom, and a tiny living room, and an even tinier kitchen. There was an attached garage, where we had to keep almost all our possessions. The house had basic furniture, and was so tiny you could barely walk. I estimate that it was about 336 sq ft. Mary, Jonny, and Rachel slept on the fold-out sofa in the living room. My parents slept in the tiny bedroom.

Earl Boyd had a bedroom in his basement, next to his garage that Jake (my brother), Daniel, and I slept in. That bedroom was next to the print shop, so I spent a lot of time there, with Elder Boyd, as he worked on the articles and magazines that he published.

Earl Boyd was in his printshop when we arrived. When we got there, he was in the middle of putting out the **Kingdom Herald**. We immediately began to help him, watching and learning about printing. After that initial exposure, he taught my father the basics of the printing trade, and I shadowed them.

He had a typesetter that used melted lead, and made slugs. He had many drawers of large type for making titles, and drawers with many symbols, decorations, and dividers that fit into the galleys to dress up the copy. After the copy was set, he would tap it down, clamp it, and do a proof. That would be proofread, and corrections were made.

Then, the galley was put into the letterpress. It was handfed. Each sheet had to be picked up, put on the table, and then the table came up and printed the ink onto the paper. The operator had to have clean hands, and had to grab the sheet by the edge, or you would get ink on your fingers and stain the next page. I remember seeing magazines arrive in our home during the early 60s that had fingerprints on the pages, and you knew the operator was sloppy! That side was allowed to dry overnight, and the next day the second side was done. I think his press run at that time was about 300 copies. That gives you an idea of the Sacred Name size at that time. I believe the **Faith** was just slightly larger in circulation than that. After the pages were all printed, they were hand assembled, saddle stapled, folded, trimmed, and mailed. It was a tedious job.

Over that summer, I often helped Earl in the print shop while my father was at work. He even had me do some typesetting, and complimented me on my accuracy for a 9 year old. One Sabbath, I was reading about the gifts of the spirit, and wrote a little article of about two paragraphs, and he published it. I was proud of the accomplishment, feeble though it was.

The Boyd's lived south of Wilder, Idaho. We went to school at Homedale, the closest town. His property bordered on the Snake River. In the spring and fall, the river was dangerous, with rushing flood waters. During the dry summer, the river level was so low, we could walk halfway across it. We couldn't swim, but we spent a lot of time in the water!

Earl and Ursula Boyd were old school all the way. They had been raised during the depression, and they gave us a new idea of frugal. On a regular basis, Earl would take us out to the local dump and we would look for anything of value. Bent cans from the stores were a favorite find. Thrown away fruit that was getting old was collected, taken home and canned. Today, as times get hard again, we see people doing dumpster diving. I understand why.

My mother didn't tell my father about getting food from the dump. She explained it away so he would not hear about it. She knew that his pride at taking care of the family would be injured if he knew where the food came from.

Earl and Ursula Boyd, had three children, Mary, Luke, David. By the time we came to stay there, Mary and Luke had just moved out. I believe that Luke was in college. David had been having some troubles with the law at that time, but we met him too when he came home to visit. During the summer, Luke was home most of the time. Over that year, we met them all, and it was a spiritual, solid family overall.

My father got a job working for a landscaper, a minimum paying job. We struggled financially. I could see the stress building on my parents, as they had no money for clothing or other needs. When my father mentioned how hard things were, Earl criticized us for eating peanut butter. My parents were stunned. That was a level of hardship and denial that they were not accustomed to in our house.

To provide milk, meat and eggs, my father bought a Jersey-Holstein cross cow that we milked twice a day. My mother milked in the morning, and my father milked in the evening. She was the first cow I ever milked. Earl had a big garden, and we helped with it. I enjoyed working in the garden. It was a different type of gardening, because it was irrigated. I enjoyed taking the shovel and guiding the water through the rows, opening up the channels so it would all receive water.

Aerial view of the Boyd house from Google earth.

The above picture taken from Google Earth, is of the Boyd property as it appears today. The large house has had an addition added since 1964, with the circular drive and garden in front of it. The little house we lived in is next to it at the corner of the circular driveway. To the left is the Snake River. The bank down to the river was very steep, and our cow used to be pastured on part of it. We spent lots of time in the summer playing in the river. It was dangerous, but times were different back then.

The Homedale Airport was across the river, and every day we could watch the airplanes coming and going. The majority of the air traffic was crop dusting, and we saw those planes come in and reload and go back out constantly.

Services at the Boyd House

The Boyd house was like a revolving door for evangelists. About every week, someone would stop in on their way past. During these visits we heard about doctrines of all kinds. The visitors were from all backgrounds, all religions, and they dabbled with doctrines of all kinds: the Friday Sabbath, 6 pm Sabbath, Sundown Sabbath, Sunday Sabbath, every day a Sabbath, Pentecostalism, HOLY Ghost, clean foods, natural foods, vegetarianism, prophecies, conspiracies, every kind of Feast day observance you can imagine, and then some.

A big topic was always prophecy. When will Yahshua return? What must we do to prepare? In my lifetime I probably heard of more than two dozen end dates for the world. My father always was hesitant to accept any of that talk. He strongly felt that, "prophecy would occur in Yahweh's time, and we should prepare ourselves for every eventuality."

Conspiracy theories abounded. The Illuminati, the Rothschilds, the Bilderbergers, the Masons, the meetings at Jekyl Island, the Banks, the Oil Giants, the Moslems, the Jews. Questions about who pulled the strings, who had the power, who Satan controlled. All these questions flowed through the Sacred name people, and still do. I have heard these theories all my life. My father heard them, but never got overly involved in any of it. He was more concerned with what must we do to be saved.

To bring in extra money, we children went to work in the orchards. Back then, when the cherries came in, the orchards paid anybody who wanted to work, by the basket and by the box for picking fruit. It was only a couple of pennies per box, but it added up if you picked fast. I made the mistake one day of drinking milk and then eating cherries while I picked. I got real sick and threw up. I learned to be more careful about what foods I mixed after that. We earned about $400 as a family picking fruit. It helped.

A very embarrassing thing happened that summer. A middle aged man who attended services sometimes at the Boyd's took my father aside, and asked for my sister's hand in marriage. My father was outraged. She was only turning 11 that fall. She looked more mature than 11, but nowhere near marriage age. Years later, another man in his 30s asked for my sister Rachel's hand in marriage, when she was only 12. People accuse the Sacred Name groups of having unstable people in them, and we saw our share.

As the summer drew to a close, the landscaping work slowed down, and my father didn't get paid for a couple of weeks. That ended that job. Out of work, my father and Earl talked frequently about the community idea in northern Idaho, and he and Earl drove north to look into that. My father, as a farmer, saw the land, and knew it was not fertile enough to support any financial endeavor, and he gave up on that idea. I could tell the stresses of finances were really telling on my parents. This is where I first heard my parents fighting. Up to this time, our home was very peaceful.

My father then heard about work in Oregon, driving truck for one of the brethren hauling lumber. He also heard about going to the dump for food, and realized that things had to change, and quickly. My parents arranged to go to the feast at Salem, Oregon, to meet the brethren there, and then my father would go back after the feast to work there over winter if it worked out.

The Calendar

The feast of 1964 was about the earliest that I can recall. That was the only feast where my birthday, September 20, fell during the feast. Usually, the feast starts at the very end of September or in early October.

It is a very common characteristic of the Sacred Name groups to try to rush the feast. Some groups have decided to lock down the feast days by following the Jews in their calculations. Some insist that we should watch for the new moon of green ears, as some interpretations of Deuteronomy 16 say. These questions came up every year, and entire books with detailed explanations of why and how the new moon of green ears should be observed have been published.

Should the Passover be on the 14th or the 15th? Should Pentecost be on Sunday or Monday or floating? Should we observe Atonement at all? Should we really keep the Feast of Tabernacles with booths? These questions were raised to critical status, and many congregations split over these questions.

My father's position has been published, so I won't review it, but remember that as a farmer, he knew how to tell if grain was ready for harvest. He found opportunities to make connections in Israel, and every year, he would talk to them and find out what the condition of the green ears was in the valley of Jericho, and on the plains around Bethlehem and west across the plains toward the Mediterranean. This kept us from keeping the feast days too early.

At first, the only method he had to predict the new moons was the farmer's almanac. In later years, we did all those calculations by computer, starting with a primitive program written for a Radio Shack model 3. I was in charge of running that program every year, and then my father and I would sit and discuss the new moons, and the feast days in depth and he would make the final decisions for the calendar.

Our method was unique. I would give him the data, and I would keep a set of data. He would sit at his desk, and I would sit across from him, and we would simultaneously work out the calendar for the whole year without talking. When we both had our answers, we would compare notes, and make the other person justify his choice. We would each listen carefully, and then discuss the differences between our views. Very soon, it was obvious which date was best, and that date would go on the calendar. I enjoyed those times, because it was so harmonious, and something we shared every year.

Chapter 5

The First Group Feast - 1964

As the summer progressed, the concern for a central feast was often discussed. The brethren in Oregon decided to sponsor the feast at Turner, Oregon, at a big wooden Gospel Tabernacle building. The brethren from Lebanon, Oregon sponsored the feast.

We packed and traveled to the feast. For some reason, Earl and Ursula did not attend. Brethren came there from Oregon, Idaho, Michigan, Missouri, and California. It was only about 50 people attending, but it was momentous.

Today, I believe that the site is currently called, "The Oregon Christian Convention Center." The old wooden Tabernacle we saw on the grounds was not used by the group for the feast, because it had been damaged in a storm. That big Tabernacle was built in 1891, and was called the Turner Memorial Tabernacle.

The below picture shows the Tabernacle after the storm of 1962. Next to it is the dormitory building that we stayed in. Today, it is called Centennial Lodge, and by the pictures, they have really improved the dormitory rooms over what they looked like when we stayed in them!

When we were there, the rooms were bare studded, with no insulation. I don't think there was a bathroom in the building. We used a chamber pot in our room. I recall the color at that time was a dull ochre, yellow color.

The old Turner Tabernacle was damaged in a bad storm in 1962, and was not ready for use yet when the feast was held on the grounds.

The dormitory that we stayed in is still standing. Our family stayed in the upstairs, in the room second from the left.

The services were held in a separate building. That building had a central kitchen for meals, with a large meeting hall attached. With only about 50 attendees, that building provided enough space for the feast of Tabernacles services and meals. Today, there is a building like it on the grounds, but I cannot tell from the pictures if it is the same structure, or if it has been rebuilt.

Behind the campground is Mill Creek. My brother Jonny, as I recall, threw one of his sneakers in the creek, and it was lost. We searched and searched for it, but we never found the sneaker. It was traumatic, because we didn't have any extra money.

We kept hearing whispers during the feast that this was the first central feast since some great tragedy had ended the feast keeping, in Michigan, but no one wanted to talk about it. I understand that it was at Camp Yah, but as I was not a witness to it, I won't pass on what I heard. I will let others answer those questions.

People questioned, was that catastrophe a sign? Was it punishment? Was it an accident? My parents felt it is best to let that question be answered by Yahweh sometime in the future when we face him. Today, they said, we need to keep the feast. Along with the tendency to add a spiritual interpretation to each event, came a tendency to ascribe a meaning to even accidents.

At this feast, all of the organizational structures that we now expect were put in place. Music nights, special music, a main sermon, some sermonettes, kid programs, and having meals as a group were all experienced here.

About the third day we were there, I realized that my father was being asked to preach every service. With his background of teaching Sunday School, he was comfortable being in front of a group. With years of listening to radio preachers, he had developed a style that was easy to listen to. He was firm and strong enough that the people felt led. So, every service, he was asked to preach. Only when he declined, did they ask anyone else.

I have to mention a highlight at that feast. We met Jim and Mary Williams. They were a very amicable young couple, fun to talk to, and to be around. She was a gifted singer, who played guitar. Almost every service, she was asked to sing songs of praise. When she produced some records in later years, almost everyone bought them, because they were so inspiring.

At this feast, there was much talk about Dugger and Dodd. Their history of the faith, **A History of the True Religion,** summarized one view of church organization, and some of those attending the feast were in communication with some of the elders in that book.

In that history, the Church of God had organized in what they believed was the biblical form. Listed in that book under the choosing of the twelve, the seventy, and the seven were 89 Elders appointed to lead.

However, it was obvious by this time, that the organization selected then had not borne fruit. It was discussed that it was time for a renewed effort by the brethren. Of those 89 elders listed, only about 10 were actively preaching. Of those, Herbert Armstrong had the largest ministry, but he was not preaching the Sacred Name. He had stayed with the Church of God doctrines primarily.

Obviously, at this feast, many of the local attendees had followed at one time, the Church of God ideas, or had attended services with some part of the Church of God. However, there were many groups around the country who did not have the Church of God background, and had no connection to C. O. Dodd. Our family, for example, had no connection to C. O. Dodd, although we did find common ground in much that he believed and wrote.

I heard discussion about the "V" believers who worked with L. D. Snow. Some had met with them, and reported that they were very firm in their belief that Yahweh should be spelled Yahveh, and they would not budge. For that matter, neither would those who gathered at the feast in Oregon, budge from their belief that the spelling should be "Yahweh".

When I read about the history of the Sacred Name Movement, I see an attempt to include every person who ever led a group, and to tie them to someone else, or to track back their origins to some common origin. I can tell you from experience, that every person we met came from some unique perspective, and had their own life experience to tell.

Strongly held beliefs from their past were brought into the Sacred Name Movement. As I shadowed the Elders, and listened, I also spent time talking with them one-on-one. Their stories are too numerous to even remember.

A common topic everyone seemed to talk about was, "How I learned the Sacred Name." Often it was a witness by a stranger, at a store, in a bus station, in a church, or in a class. Sometimes it was when they came across the Sacred Name in a book. Sometimes it was a pamphlet they found, or a magazine that got mailed to them. Sometimes it seemed an accident, or was it?

Another favorite topic was personal appearance. How should women dress? What was modest garb? Can a woman wear pants? Should a man wear a beard? What about head coverings? These topics were discussed in that feast in 1964. And, they have been discussed at **every** feast, from 1964 to date.

It is good for each person to seek truth, to find ideas to think about. That is commendable. However, very often, the same old doctrinal questions were raised by people who just wanted to fight, or stir up a fight, and sit back and watch the drama unfold as the congregation disintegrated.

There is a big difference between the question, "What must I do to be saved?" and the approach, "What must we demand from others?" If the person is only worried about his own salvation, the discussion is never heated or confused. Maybe the answers, privately given by a range of believers may differ, but the inquirer can hear, study, and decide between those answers on his own.

I have seen all my life that if the emphasis is on what we should demand from others, then it gets heated, and dogmatic, and angers arise.

At this feast, we felt a true unity of purpose. The approach was, "What must I do to be saved?" Therefore, the Bible studies throughout the feast broadened the view and informed each person in attendance. When we left that feast, we felt invigorated. We were determined to do better in our spiritual life.

As an overall observation about feasts. The first one in a location was usually the best. After the first feast, later feasts at that site see discouragements come in, dissent comes in, and people leave discouraged, not inspired. This is human nature. My father saw this tendency in the Sacred Name Movement, and from 1969 through 1979, he kept the focus of the feast on the personal question, "What must I do to be saved?" After 1980, things changed.

Should We Move to Oregon?

After the feast ended, we said our goodbyes to all, and drove back to Idaho. Immediately after resting from the trip, my father turned around and went to Oregon again to do a trial period working for one of the brethren. He drove truck for them, hauling lumber, and spent the time with the brethren around Lebanon, Oregon, getting to know them. He always had a soft spot for those families in Oregon after that, even though the job did not fulfill his expectations.

About 1966, they sent him a set of ordination credentials, out of the blue, and he had two ordination certificates under glass on the right side of his desk, and the under glass on the pull-out tray of his desk in later years. Those certificates reminded him of the past, had the beloved elders he worked with in the early years.

He saw that trying to get re-established in Oregon would be expensive. The job didn't pay enough to cover that expense, and he kept asking himself, "Why did I move to Idaho?" He had moved to help Earl Boyd, and although he had learned a great deal about the Sacred Name Movement on the West Coast, he saw that there was not a strong movement happening, like he had seen growing in the East. He wanted to be part of a dynamic growing group of True Worshipers, who were living out the Book of Acts in the End Time. He didn't see that in Idaho, or on the West Coast at that time.

I turned 10 during that feast in Oregon. After the feast, we returned to Idaho, and I was back to school in fifth grade. That was a hard time. My teacher was an ex-Marine sergeant who believed in strong corporal punishment. He had a big wooden paddle with holes drilled in it, and if any of the children were out of line, they were spanked hard.

One day, after lunch, several of us were in the classroom talking, and that was against the rules. He suddenly came in and took out the students that he saw talking. I was not chosen, but I felt bad because I had been talking before he came in. My best friend was a boy named Isaac, and he got paddled, but he never gave me up as being one of those talking.

This school figured greatly in our history, because of the feasts. When we took time off in Pa for religious holidays, we got full credit if we did the work and handed it in when we got back from the feast trips. At Homedale, we got our assignments, did our homework, and handed it in. When we got our report cards for the first quarter, we all had zeros for the quarter. My father was irate. He went to the Principal and the Superintendent, and they would not budge. If you were gone, you got zeros.

That was the final straw. My parents decided to pack and move back to Pennsylvania. His boss still owed him money, so to settle up, he gave my father a plywood and frame, closed trailer to move with. We loaded everything up again, including all the jars of canned fruit, and jelly that my mother had canned. Those boxes were heavy for the car, and my father was careful to put that weight, and his books, over the single axle, to help the car balance the load. We headed east.

Moving Back to Pennsylvania

It was a hard trip, because money was so short. We slept in the car, in roadside rests on the ground, but not in any motels on that trip. Mostly, we drove and drove. We didn't make any special stops in tourist locations. My mother was pregnant, and that made the trip hard for her.

In Iowa, on a lonely stretch of road, the left rear tire blew on the car. My father, as an experienced driver, held the heavy car and trailer load, and brought it safely to the side of the road. He unhitched the trailer, emptied the trunk, and began to jack up the car. When he got the car as high as it would go, he took off the flat and tried to put on the spare. The car was not quite high enough. He raised it again, to the limit of the jack, and it still needed a fraction of an inch.

My father asked me to lift the tire onto the hub as he pushed down the last and final click on the jack. I picked up the tire, and just as it was going on the hub, the jack broke and down came the car. My dad jumped frantically toward me because he feared my arms were trapped under the collapsed car. He rejoiced to see that I had picked the tire up with my hands on the bottom side of the tire, and the car just drove my arms down, and bruised them, without breaking them.

So there we sat, on a lonely stretch of Iowa highway, with no jack. No cars were passing. We were many miles from the nearest town. Suddenly, from behind us, a pickup drove up, passed us, and saw we had a problem. Two farmers sat in the pickup, and they got out and asked if they could help. My father showed them what happened, and they smiled and said, "Well, what do you know, we just bought a new jack this morning, here it is," as they got it out of the bed of the truck. They helped my father jack up the car and install the tire.

Before they left, my father asked to buy the jack. They sold it to him at cost, got back in their truck, turned around on the road, and drove back the way they came. Ever since then, my parents said they had to be angels.

The Bethel Farmhouse

We arrived back in Pennsylvania and stayed at my Grandpa Foreman's house for a few days. During that time, my parents found a house for rent. It was a huge, old stone farmhouse with no improvements, except a bathroom and electricity. It had no central heat, no insulation, the snow blew through the window cracks in the winter. In other words, it was fairly typical for a farmhouse in 1964. The rent was $36 per month. Later, when it got raised to $38 and then $42, my parents fussed about the expensive rent. With that, we got a large garden, about an eight acre meadow, and a small barn.

That house was over 2,000 sq ft, and after the mobile home, and the tiny house in Idaho, it felt like a mansion! We put a coal/wood stove in each downstairs room, and kept nice and warm. Some of my fondest memories of growing up were of that house. Whenever I walk into a house, and smell the smells of cooking and feel the warm rooms, I am taken quickly back to those days. About that time, plastic film became available, and we bought plastic, and covered all the windows in the winter to save heat. That was before insulated glass and vinyl windows.

My father took a job again driving truck for Gotwals, and quickly recovered our finances. Micah was born shortly after we moved there, on December 16, 1964. For the rest of that winter, and into the summer, we re-established ties to all the local brethren, meeting some families that had begun worshiping with the Sacred Name Believers. Among them were the Eberly's and the Bichers. We also met a baker from Schoeneck who made the absolute best seven grain all natural bread. We also met the Dintiman's and the Blouchs at Highspire for Passover.

Many of the brethren were serious about health foods. My parents began to get **Organic Gardening** and **Prevention** magazine about this time. We tried hard to eat good, nutritious food. We sprouted grains, ate lots of salads, raised and preserved all we could of our own unprocessed foods.

Preparing for the feast always meant carrying a note to the school teacher and principal informing them of our observance of the feasts, and telling them of the days we were gone. We always asked for the homework, and we would sit at a table every day of the feast, and do our homework. After the feast, we would give the packet of work to the teacher, and get credit for what we did. Only once in my school years did the teacher say, "Forget about it… we'll worry about that when you get back. Have a great time!" Usually, we got detailed lists of every assignment, and we had to do them for grades.

A larger implication from feast observance was that every year, the students would re-align their friendships after the summer break, and re-establish their old friendships. So, school would start after Labor Day, and we would go for two weeks, and then be gone for two weeks. By the time we got back, all the friendship groups were set, and we were outsiders. It is hard to measure the impact this has on a child.

Chapter 6

The Feast of 1965

That summer, Paul and Aggie stopped by with their mini-bus, and we had a great time visiting with them for three days. Then, they left, as was Paul's rule. During that time, they told us of a group in Missouri that were thinking of having a feast that was more central than Oregon.

Everyone agreed that having the feast in Oregon had been a good thing, to get the feasts going again, in a new setting away from the stigma of the feast in Michigan that ended central feasts. But now it was time to have a more central feast since those brethren from the east could not travel all the way to Oregon.

The talk throughout that summer, with every service, and every visit, was, "We need to evangelize." My parents made plans to travel to Nevada, Missouri ,for the feast. They rented a fold down camper trailer, and made all the arrangements to be gone for two weeks.

When we arrived there, we saw that instead of having a campground, that the brethren were going to hold the feast in a house in town. They greeted us warmly, and the men helped my father pull the camper into the back yard of the house. There we set up camp, and spent the week. A couple of the single men had small tents they also set up in the yard, some of the women stayed in the house, some families stayed at hotels.

It seems that every feast has a theme, and this feast centered around the need to evangelize. There was a lot of talk about advertising, revivals, evangelism, teaching programs, and how to bring people to know the truth. It was clear, with about 40 people at the feast. That this was a tiny movement.

Attending there is Missouri were some from Michigan. Pearl Smith lived up to her name. She was a real pearl. We all loved her. As a senior woman, she was truly a paragon, and a leader and good influence for the younger women. She held most of the kid classes, and really taught us with sincerity and love. Joseph Owsen was also there. I still think of him as Joseph Owsinski, his Polish name. He was a pleasant, almost jolly man, that people gravitated toward.

During the first Sabbath, he sat on the steps outside the kitchen, and I was hanging around, and he asked me a question. He asked, "Could I list all the feast days?" He promised that if I could, he would give me a dime. I listed them off for him, and he was very pleased, and dug out a dime. When he held it out for me, I refused to reach for it. He was puzzled, and I told him that it was the Sabbath, and we were not to buy or sell, so I could not sell him the answers, I could only do it for free. He was shocked, amazed, and made a point to go straight to my father, and complimented him on his raising, and his teaching of his children.

On a regular basis, my parents were complimented on how well we behaved. In the previous generation, strict family rules were expected, and children were generally expected to behave. As things loosened in the 60s, and general rebellion among the youth was common, our obedience and respect were refreshing to the old folks. As the years went by, people began to question why we were so good, and people assumed that my parents were abusive and beat us into submission. That is far from the truth.

We had rules, strict rules, but they were not excessive. They were clear, and respect was demanded. We did not have to say "Yes, sir," or "Yes, maam." Our respect was to listen, learn, and help.

Later, when I heard parents demanding "Yes, sir," or "Yes, maam." I also noticed that many of the children did it, but mockingly. We were genuinely respectful, or we were quickly punished.

Every Sabbath, we had studies as a family, and my parents would ask us questions to make sure we were listening. We were asked to recite the books of the Bible, the names of the Patriarchs, the names of the Apostles, the Ten Commandments, the Feast Days, the rules for clean foods. All that was second nature for us.

Again, at this feast in 1965, most of the services were preached by my father.

Also attending at that feast was a family from Michigan named Vlad. Danny Vlad was a very friendly, outgoing man. He brought his two sons, Mike and Mark. I don't remember if their mother came along. We spent a lot of time with the Vlad boys, went for walks, sat with them at services, and saw them at various meetings over the next two or three years. I heard that the boys attended Spring Vale Academy, a Church of God, Seventh Day, school in Owosso, Michigan, and that Mike became a pastor for the Church of God, Seventh Day, Denver. Mark Vlad at one time was at Rock City, Ill. They were a very spiritual family, as time has proven.

In Michigan, Elder William Bishop and Elder Bowen were well known, and although I don't remember Elder Bishop, Elder Bowen came to the feast in Missouri. He was a quiet man, and had a fascination with Hebrew. I had the impression that he was a former Jew, but maybe I got that impression because to understand the Sacred Names, you have to study some Hebrew. He gave me a card with his address on it, and we began to correspond. In the summer of 1966, he sent me a Hebrew Psalter, and a Hebrew OT. They were tiny, with tiny print, as so many books were at that time. I still have them.

This was the first feast that I saw Pentecostalism within the Sacred Name Believers. Although Earl Boyd was rather Pentecostal, and spoke often in tongues, he was rather calm and quiet with his utterances. However, here at the feast, while the men were gone one afternoon, and the women were cooking, one of the older women attendees went into the room we used for services, and began to stomp, speak in tongues, and receive prophetic messages.

She was shouting about the need for us to wear white, and to worship barefoot. She believed that only wearing white (the robes of righteousness) and being barefoot to show our humility in Yahweh's presence would Yahweh be pleased. She also saw a need for more open displays of tongues in the assembly, and felt the congregation was suppressing the spirit.

This display went on for well over an hour, as she was shouting and screaming, stomping her feet on the wooden floors, and gasping for breath. Soon, the city police came to the door, because the neighbors thought someone was being killed. Even at 11 years old, that didn't make sense to me, as the Spirit of Yahweh was a spirit of peace, and this type of emotional out of control display was alien to our worship.

Pearl Smith was there the entire feast. She taught during services at times, but she always did it sitting down. She taught that the elders should be men. She respected diverse gender roles. But, she had such good insight, that we all viewed her as a prophetess, such as Deborah in the Bible. Sister Smith taught the children's classes the same way, sitting down. She sat and worked with the women in the kitchen and taught the younger women how to be good wives and mothers. I am sure that she was a model for my mother later in life.

Near the end of the feast, as the group discussed how to go forward, and how to evangelize, it was Pearl Smith who began to talk about how the evidence is right before them all. She drew their attention to my father, and told them that in her opinion, Yahweh had brought Mr. Meyer into the faith for a reason. She reminded them about how good of a teacher he was, and how he could inspire people to seek truth, and to do better with their spiritual life. She then suggested that they ordain Jacob O. Meyer.

As I recall, there were four elders that laid hands on him, and she did too. She may have even brought forward the Olive Oil. None of us were surprised that she joined in. No one pushed her away, she was welcome to participate. After the ordination, I didn't hear any person being shocked or critical about her participation. She was a good, kind, strong believer, a prophetess you could call her, why should she not stand in support of his ordination, and add her hands to the ordination? When he was ordained, he called us all forward, and as a family, we all stood with him. After the prayer, he took of the oil they had poured over his head, and he put some of it on my mother's head, and the head of each of his children. The picture below is taken in the exact spot where he was ordained.

The children are by age and size: Mary, Joseph, Jacob, Daniel, Jonathan, Rachel, and Micah in my father's arms. I am standing by my in the second row, on the right.

The Meyer family at the feast of 1965. Elder Jacob O Meyer (holding Micah), Ruth Meyer, Mary, me (Joseph), Jacob, Daniel, Jonathan, and Rachel.

It was about 20 years later that I first heard the criticism that a woman had ordained my father. That criticism stunned me, because his ordination was approved by the entire group: men and women. What is ordination? Yahweh ordains, and the actions of the individual are the proof. In reality, all we humans can do is to put forward someone to show our approval and selection. It is Yahweh who ordains. Many men are anointed, very few are faithful, and very few act like they have been ordained to serve Yahweh for the rest of their lives.

Evangelism Begins

After the feast, Elder Meyer felt strongly that his ordination was a sign from Yahweh that he had a job to do, to tell others about the truth of the Sacred Name and the doctrines of the Bible. I remember how he and my mother were so inspired. He explained to all of us that just as he had been ordained, he had put the oil on our heads too, and we now also had a responsibility to do our best to serve Yahweh.

We returned to Bethel, to the stone farmhouse. Immediately, my father was approached by both Paul Kwiatkowski and Florence Waggy from Baltimore. They asked him to take over the radio broadcast on WBMD Baltimore.

Sister Waggy was a former Seventh Day Adventist member, as I recall. She was a retired nurse, and was totally blind, and living in a nursing home that I believe she owned or co-owned. When we first met her, she had a mind that was as sharp as a tack, as they say. For hours, my parents would sit and discuss the Bible with her. She was funding the broadcast on WBMD every Sabbath day at noon, to help to spread the Sacred Name.

Paul Kwiatkowski was doing the broadcast, and it was very unprofessional. He and Aggie would sit by the tape recorder, and do a little study, both of them talking, singing and praying. Paul did not feel that he was the right person for the task. He called my father and asked if he would take it over. At that same time, Sister Waggy called and asked him to take over the recording of the broadcast.

I remember that as they talked about plans for the future, my father was very clear that he wanted to evangelize, he did not want to make another church or have membership to worry about and keep in line. He just wanted to preach the glad tidings to the world.

Many times in later years, as we sat in his office, he would remind me of those days, and how uncomplicated they were. He often said he would rather have been a preacher, an evangelist, who could sit in the back and criticize others. He always said that with a smile, as we knew that by nature he was not overly critical. Sometimes he was blunt, sometimes taken as harsh, but when things were going smoothly, he was very easy to get along with.

Later on, I heard others say that things went smoothly when things went my father's way. They said that if things didn't go his way, that he became upset. I guess that was true too. Of course, I saw him when he was not in charge. I saw him when he could just teach and preach, without having to be in charge. And, in those circumstances, he was more than willing to let things go the way the leader of the congregation chose to run things. He was not a compulsive organizer, but he had little patience for confusion and constant bickering over doctrines. When we visited congregations that had diverse ideas, such as A.B. Traina, my father did not raise those doctrines to provoke the leader.

But if a congregation we were visiting was disintegrating due to lack of leadership that was able to quiet the situation down, then my father did feel compelled to step up, if others supported him, and encouraged him.

Below is a picture of Elder Meyer walking Miss Waggy to the car in Maryland after services. We had been visiting this small congregation west of Baltimore on a fairly regular basis, and this was their new meeting hall. Upstairs, as I recall, the Pastor lived. I think his name was Pastor Gibson, but I am not sure.

1966. Elder Meyer walking Ms Waggy to the car to take her back to the nursing home.

As soon as the agreement was made to have my father do the radio broadcasts, my parents went to Sears, and bought a small recorder that produced the same small 3 inch reels of tape recordings that Paul Kwiatkowski was producing. They quickly learned from the station, that the recording was too weak. The sound circuits were amateur, and they needed a new machine. My parents used their tax return that year, and went back to Sears, and bought their best recorder. It had much better sound, and could record or play a 7 inch reel.

The Sacred Name Broadcast

Usually, on a Sunday morning, my father would have the broadcast ready. He had an old Underwood typewriter that he would use to type up the 15 minute broadcast. It usually took four pages of double spaced type to fill 15 minutes. He would end the broadcast without his address or phone number. This was pure evangelism. There was no attempt to build a group.

As the name of the show illustrates, it was all centered around the need for us to use the Sacred Name. Program after program looked at this topic from every angle. Even a program about the feast days tied into the need to worship Yahweh properly, on the right day, and using his correct name.

He did not give an address or phone number on the initial programs. However, very soon, people began calling the station to find out who this was, and how to reach him. One of those inquirers was Iona McConnell. The station finally called and asked him to put his name and address on the tape, so they would not be bothered by so many phone calls. From the first broadcast where he identified hiimself, he ended the show by asking them to write to "The Assemblies of Yahweh, P.O. Box C, Bethel, Pa, 19507. And may Yahweh bless you abundantly." He used that same ending for his broadcasts all his life.

Eddie and Iona McConnell from Baltimore accepted the Sacred Names, were baptized later that year, and followed the Assemblies of Yahweh, and attended services and Feast Days, as they could, all their lives. Many others from the Baltimore area learned of the Sacred Names through this broadcast.

Each Sunday morning, my father would prepare to record his broadcast. He usually recorded early in the morning, before the children got up. He would set up the recorder on the living room coffee table, and my mother would sit on the sofa and do the recording. He ran the microphone cord to the desk, and he would sit there behind the desk, and read the script.

Because he had listened to so many radio preachers, he knew how to properly enunciate and how to accent his voice so it carried. When I first saw the physical effort he put into every word, it stunned me. But, I realized that when recorded, that was necessary to get a clear sound.

On a regular basis, the neighbor's dog would begin barking. I don't know if it was the sound of the emphatic recording voice coming from our house, or what it was, but this old Beagle would begin howling and yipping. It was my job to go out there, and keep him quiet. So, I would sit by his dog house, on the dirt, and scratch his ears and talk to him, to keep him occupied, so the howling would not get on the tape.

Not having a studio, unplanned noised like airplanes, fire trucks, etc happened occasionally, and then the tape would have to be backed up and either started over , or a cut in would have to be attempted. My father liked having the entire 15 minutes recorded in one session, without a break. That is why he typed it up, so he would not have a lapse of concentration and lose his place. He did not want any uhs or ahhs interrupting the listener. He strived to make the program professional right from the start.

At this time, we heard of others who were putting radio shows on local radio stations. We heard of a broadcast from Michigan. We heard of one in Alabama. We heard of one in Texas. This was fantastic, and encouraging, to see so many acting on the desire to get the truth out to the world. My parents did not view this as competition, they realized that there were many men working in the harvest, and it was a huge world, and every bit of help was needed.

Just before the Feast of Tabernacles, we were invited to go to Irvington, NJ, for the Day of Atonement. The services were to be held in the church that A.B.Traina held services in. Although he did not believe in keeping the Day of Atonement, he had agreed to let the brethren of his congregation use the church.

During the service, he came in and began a very loud argument with his own members about how his people should respect him, even if they did not agree with him. He said they knew he did not believe we should fast on Atonement, and yet they came into his church on the Day of Atonement, and disrespected him. He did not confront my father, in particular, but he asked us all to leave. My father did not argue with him over it. We thought it had all been approved. We moved to a local home for the rest of the day. It was quite emotional.

(I had a similar event happen to me in 1984 when I was invited to preach in a house usually used by the Church of God, Seventh Day, on the Island of Guadeloupe. I was asked to leave the house, and the entire congregation went with me to another house. They kept me up all night asking questions. Later, I baptized almost the whole congregation into the Sacred Names.)

Ironically, when that Irvington, N.J. church was discontinued about 1971, the piano and the benches were given the Bethel congregation and were in our meeting hall for years.

At every feast and at every meeting, people expressed hope for a huge conversion. Just as we had gotten on fire about the truth of the Sacred Name, and felt a need for believing and using it, we all hoped that one day the world would wake up and accept this truth.

Many Sacred Name preachers said during their sermons that they hoped for the day when all the organized churches were using Yahweh's name, and there would be no need for the Sacred Name movement. It was a common hope that our local churches would supply the fellowship and leadership that we all needed.

Every year, people would bring evidence that the Sacred Names were becoming more familiar and more accepted. Magazine articles using Yahweh's name were circulated. If any leader in religion used it on a broadcast or interview, it was talked about. Then in 1966, the Jerusalem Bible was published. This filled everyone with hope. A major Bible, published by the Catholic Church, used the Sacred Names!

This fervor grew through the late 1960s, but about 1971, the tide changed. The established religions formed a resistance to the Sacred Names. Articles against using it began to be published in groups that we came out of, dashing the hopes that they would change and we could go back to our home churches. Some of the articles were harsh, some just ridiculed the truth of the Sacred Names, some were outrageous in their attempt to discredit the Sacred Name believers.

We always hoped for a champion. We hoped that some prominent leader with a broad following and great credibility would step forward, and tell the world that this is the truth! However, it never happened. As the years went on, the witnessing and evangelism grew, but only a small number of people stepped forward and followed the belief that the Sacred Names were important.

Many congregations that had 30 members in 1966 still have 30 members today. Groups have arisen and fallen when sin and error entered in. People would get on fire, full of inspiration, and then they would get tired and disappear. The leaders of the past have passed away, and many times there was no one to take their place. There is a difference between an inspiring evangelist and an administrator. Many groups became led by administrators, and the growth stopped.

All of these factors were being seen already in 1966, and it worried the leaders of the Sacred Name Movement. What could they do to stabilize and strengthen the Sacred Name Movement?

Chapter 7

The Feasts of 1966 - 1967

As we readied for the Feast of Tabernacles, I heard all of these thoughts were being discussed by letter and by phone as my father communicated with leaders around the country. Plans were made to hold the Feast of Tabernacles at Jackson's Gap, Alabama.

Pastor Bob McBride was a fairly young man, and had a property and a church building. He had a steady demeanor, and could inspire people to try harder in their spiritual walk. And, he was reaching out to local congregations in his area to tell them of the truth, and was inviting them in to Bible studies and services. The congregation was growing, and this was the hope for the future that all the leaders of the Sacred Name movement had in their hearts.

When we arrived at Jackson's Gap, we set up our camper, and soon other campers and tents were being set up in the pine forest around the church. Looking back, this was the first feast where a large number of the congregants camped out.

Camping near our camper and tent were a family from Michigan, named Robert Young. He and my father spent a lot of time together that feast, discussing the Bible, sorting out what doctrines they agreed on, and where they disagreed in belief and practice. Many of the others joined in, including Mike Olyphant, and the Halls.

The families that attended this feast tended to be young. This inspired us, as at previous meetings and feasts so many of the leaders were old and obviously tired of the fight. Here we saw many young men, willing to step out and evangelize the truth. They were men with vision, ambition, and dynamic personalities. It inspired all of us.

Good Cooking, Bad Gossip

I must say that the food at this feast was the best up to that time. At home we had good country cooking, and I learned that down south, they do the same. Corn bread, biscuits, fresh, buttery mashed potatoes, fried chicken. I remember the food well. For breakfast, I learned to enjoy Grits. That was a new taste for me, and I still enjoy them to this day.

At this feast, I saw a need for working in the kitchen. Although there were plenty of cooks, I could see that the cooks were having to wash up the pots and pans and dishes after hours of cooking. I made it a point every day to go back to the kitchen, and help out with the cleanup after every meal, and sometimes before the meal I would help wash pots. It cut into my social time with the other children, but many times I was back there with the adults, and I could hear their conversation and discussion, and that made it worthwhile.

However, a lot of what I heard over the years in the kitchens won't be put in this book. This is about my memories, therefore, my observations. I must say, I heard some juicy gossip in the kitchens over the years! But such idle talk was just gossip, and was probably a mix of truth and error, so it doesn't need to be repeated. We all have a story, and sometimes those stories are exaggerated or misconstrued. If you listen to gossip in kitchens, you would learn to believe the worst of everyone!

I remember one time when Elder Clyde Wilson walked in on some members who were gossiping, and he listened a few minutes by the door before they realized he was there. He came into the room, and proceeded to gently reprimand all of those involved because gossip is always damaging, and was in violation of Matthew 18. I bring this up, because at every feast, we always heard a lot of gossip! It is just human nature.

Today, we have the internet, and the gossip still goes on. I have seen some of the blogs, and cannot believe the meanness and harshness and vindictiveness I see there. Our family was taught in the Brethren way, to be quiet, and to mind your own business, and not to spread or listen to idle gossip. If you didn't see it or hear it, you should not get involved, and you should never repeat it.

In 1966, one of the lead cooks was Mrs. Hall. I remember seeing her working in the kitchen, and hearing the younger women gossiping, and she would just shake her head to discourage it. If they saw her, they would quickly change the subject. It seems at every feast, there were one or two older men or women who consistently tried to keep the gossip in check.

How much damage has been done over the decades by gossip in the Sacred Name Movement? I am sure a great deal of damage has been done. We don't know the lives of those who come to feasts, good or bad. Our human curiosity drives us to learn about others, and too often we try to connect dots that do not exist, or we fill in and color the picture in ways it should not be. The biggest problem with a small group is that the emphasis can be put on the individual, and that leads to gossip.

Pentecostal Disruptions

One night, the same woman who disrupted the feast in Nevada, Missouri, the year before, interrupted services by doing the same thing she did in Missouri. She got up during the sermon, and began to march up and down the aisle, at first agreeing with the pastor, and raising a lot of amens and hallelujah's!

Then she began to digress onto other holiness subjects: white robes, bare feet, how women dress, evil thoughts, etc. She got louder and louder, and would not stop. Half of her shouting was in English, half was in an unknown tongue. When a couple of the men tried to stop her, she shook them off and continued stomping up and down the aisle. It went on and on, and most were uncomfortable in the room. She was in a total frenzy. Gradually, the mothers took their small children out, and then whole families left, and soon only a couple of the men sat there, discouraged. The service was over, finally she got exhausted, and left, and the men got up and turned out the lights for the night.

Events like this were discouraging to all. People asked, how can we grow and appear to be serious about our salvation, when interruptions like this happen? How do visitors see us when one person can tear apart a service, stop a sermon, and destroy our peace? Each congregation over the years had to deal with this type of question. The way the congregation answered it determined to a great extent their future. If they opened the door to all displays labeled as spiritual, then the church began to look like a free-for-all. If they squashed all displays, they became so rigid that people were not inspired.

Most fell in between somewhere. Special music nights were held to allow free expression. Services of testimony were held to allow others beside the pastor to speak and talk about issues. Informal sing-a-longs were held outside at picnic benches. All of these devices have been used over the years to allow persons free expression while keeping order.

It is difficult to administer during a feast. The leaders advertised the feast far and wide, and invited all to attend. So, all types of people did attend. All types of doctrines were brought in.

At one of our Assemblies of Yahweh feasts in Missouri, I believe it was 1979, a man from Texas was scheduled to give a special song. His introduction to that song lasted over an hour. I was the song leader, and I got up and moved to the side to encourage him to get on with it, but I couldn't get his attention, he avoided my eye contact, and refused to acknowledge me. He also refused to meet the eyes of my father sitting right in front of him. The congregation was getting very restless, and something had to be done, as there was no end in sight for his impromptu sermon. We didn't want to just drag him off the podium and cause further embarrassment.

I was sitting on the podium behind him with Elder Donald Mansager. Elder Mansager kept whispering to me, "Can't you stop him? What can we do?" Finally, I said, "Can we give him a note?" Elder Mansager wrote up a quick note on a page from his little notebook, and tore it out and handed it to me. It said, "You are speaking too long, wrap it up, NOW."

I handed him the note, and he paused, read it, quickly sang his song, and left the podium. After the service, My father and Elder Mansager took him aside and talked to him about proper decorum and the order of service.

The Elders had a real juggling act to perform, to keep the feasts running smoothly. Eventually, as I said, they all built strategies to handle such situations. Agree with those strategies or not, something had to be done to be able to hold the feasts. One of the most effective strategies was for the elders to test the people out during the year in local settings, and only those people who showed good common sense throughout the year were given responsibilities.

However, some of the attendees came from areas with no pastor, and no services to test them. Recognizing this, those potential leaders would be given small responsibilities, and they were evaluated by those efforts.

By the end of the feast of 1966, everyone was feeling very inspired. For the last Sabbath, a group came in who almost doubled the group! L.F. Wilds, Paul Wilds, and Wm Bodine all came to worship and meet the brethren. I believe they all preached at least a sermonette, but what stirred us all up was the music. When the Wilds families sang, they were good singers. They had their guitars and tambourines along, and they used a lot of emotion. The congregation really got stirred up.

Wm Bodine was a lively speaker. He really preached about the need for personal salvation. Even though he had doctrinal differences with some of the other pastors, he set that aside, and preached on common topics that inspired everyone. It was only years after his death that I learned that he differed on a number of doctrines, some of them quite significant.

Some pastors can set aside their pet doctrines. Some feel a need to push them in your face every time they see you. I remember a sermonette Elder Bodine preached one time about grinding an ax. He talked about how some just grind away, and grind away, over and over, like they could not help themselves, and eventually they ruin their own ax! We got the message. But it was only years later that I understood he was also using himself as an example. There are more important issues on the table than our pet doctrines. We need to be concerned with our salvation, and our personal lives. Will we be pleasing to Yahweh when we stand in front of him?

During this feast of 1966, the people really drew together in unity. There was not a competitive spirit there. When we left, we were all filled with the need to go out and preach the word. At the last service, Matthew 28:19-20 was read at the last service, "Go you therefore, and make disciples of all the nations, immersing them into the name of the father and of the son, and of the holy spirit: teaching them to observe all things whatever I commanded you." The final song was, "Til We Meet Again."

This combination has been used at almost every feast I have been at since then. It never fails to raise tears in all our eyes as we look around the friends, new and old, that we shared the feast with. We never know who will pass on until next year. We had a wonderful feast. We are filled with zeal to go out and show others the path to salvation, to encourage those who are struggling in their personal walks, but we know for some of us, the time may be short. We never know when our time is up, and we will be laid to rest. These are emotional thoughts as we leave the feast.

I remember as we left the feast, it began to rain. It was a cold rain as we drove through northern Alabama, and I put my forehead against the cold car window glass and felt so sad, thinking about those we left, and would not see until next year.

Growing Pains

Throughout the winter and into the summer of 1967, we heard reports from all over the U.S. about progress being made in conversions to the Sacred Name. The Sacred Name Broadcast was expanded to more stations, and letters and contributions came from all over the US, Mexico, and Canada. All the money was being channeled into paying for radio time. My father signed contracts on faith, hoping that brethren would continue to contribute through the next year. If the contributions would have dried up, he would have been personally responsible to pay them, and it would have been impossible. It was a stress that constantly weighed on him.

I am sure that many of the attempts to evangelize in other areas fell apart due to the stresses of money and support. It took a fairly large congregation to carry the monthly expenses of a radio broadcast. Also, the stresses of making the broadcasts and answering mail, and talking to inquirers definitely puts stress on a family.

My father was still working full time, although he shifted his hours to second shift, so he could be at home to work in the ministry, and make business calls during office hours. He was basically working two jobs, and with preaching and counseling on the Sabbath, he was probably working 100 hours a week. Our family life was minimal. I also saw the stresses from Idaho kept coming back in my parent's relationship. It is not healthy for a couple to be struggling financially, trying to raise their family, and on top of that, being out in front of the public so much.

I believe that much of the talk about my father's harshness derives entirely from the stresses that all this work and the lack of money put on him and the family. He had no savings, he had put it all into the ministry. When our car was hit from behind in a snow storm, instead of buying a good, new car, he bought a second hand clunker. That gave trouble of course, and had to go back to the dealer.

He got a good 1959 station wagon, and drove that for two years. Then, one morning, he decided that he would take us boys fishing. My uncle Jim was going to come along. We left home in a deep fog, and a half mile from home, a drunk came down our lane, and hit us head on. The car caught on fire. I flew from the third seat over the second, and hit my back on the front seat. That was the start of my back injuries.

The drunk kid was in the military, home on leave, and drinking all night. He had no assets, and our settlement by today's standards was miniscule. The insurance co paid us $125 for my injuries. My father had smashed his teeth on the steering wheel, and broken his foot, and he got $250. The car was destroyed, and he did get that paid off.

But, that left us without a car again. Thankfully, my father talked to a relative who worked at Keller Brother's Ford, and heard about a like-new station wagon that one of the owners had just traded in. He bought that 1964 Ford Country Squire Station Wagon, and that car carried my father on ministerial trips and our family to feasts and services all over the country for about six years.

However after the bad accident, like so many people struggle in religion, we questioned Yahweh. We asked as Job did, "Why did this happen to us?" Too often, we come up with the wrong answers. Yahweh told Job not to question him, as he is far above us. Sometimes things happen beyond our comprehension and beyond our control.

As a result of that accident, my father felt guilty for not working in the ministry on that Sunday morning the way that he usually did. He felt that if he would have been working at his desk, he would not have put us all in danger.

For the next five years, all of my father's time was devoted to earning a living, and doing the work of the ministry, for which he got no pay. It strongly advanced the ministry of the Assemblies of Yahweh, but our family suffered for that decision. We took no vacations. We spent no time for relaxation. We rationalized it as a necessary sacrifice to Yahweh.

During this summer, I had begun to advance my fascination with biology and the study of human systems, and was voraciously reading everything I could get my hands on about medicine. I decided that I wanted to be a doctor. I talked to my parents about it one Sabbath, and they were emphatic that we should rely on Yahweh for healing, that doctors worked on the Sabbath, and that if I went to medical school, that I would have to touch dead cadavers, and that would violate the command not to touch unclean bodies.

That ended my career as a doctor. As the years went by, I learned how the Seventh Day Adventists encouraged their youth to go into medicine, because it was the ultimate good deed, to preserve the life that Yahweh gave us. This seemed to be a more responsible interpretation than the interpretation of the Sacred Name Movement.

At this time, we also began to hear the expression from my father, "What will people think?" We used to joke about it when he was not around. His reaction to being in the public eye was to become more strict. I have seen this in many others throughout my life. As a person is given more responsibility over a congregation, they tend to become more strict on themselves, their family, and demanded stricter obedience from others.

This decision not to allow me to be a doctor taught me lessons. The Bible did not say I could not be a doctor. The Bible had commands that were interpreted to restrict me from being a doctor. It was all interpretation. Later, when I was an elder, I began to resist going two and three steps beyond what the Bible says, and adding to the Word. Of course, when I began to question interpretations and "policies," it got me in trouble.

I have read blogs about "damage" done to children raised in religion, and particularly in the Sacred Name movement. Most of that kind of talk on the surface sounds like a lot of whining. I never flet that way. But the impact of decisions by parents in how their children live can have permanent impacts. These decisions are life changing, and I understand when a child without choice has his life thrown in an unproductive direction due to the parent's interpretation and gets bitter. You can certainly label it as damage, if you compare what their life could have been. But I digress, and I apologize.

The Six Day War

Later that summer, a shocking event happened. Israel was attacked by the Arab nations around them, with the intent of total annihilation. The Six Day War started on June 5, 1967. For six days, we were glued to the radio, not knowing if Israel would survive.

The impact of this event on the Sacred Name Movement was immense. First of all, A.N.Dugger was publishing the **Mt Zion Reporter** from Jerusalem, and we all worried about him and the brethren there. Secondly, with years of prophecy talk in the services, this war became a key starting point for the countdown to the end of the age. Some began to prophecy that the world would end in 1973, some had already published that this age of man would end in 1975. The war in 1967 fueled emotions that these prophets were on the right track. Young people my age wondered if we should even bother going to college, since we may never graduate anyway.

Well, we know how all that worked out for the prophets. By the year 1973, dates and interpretations were changing quickly, and some preachers lost their credibility due to things they had published.

Herbert Armstrong was one of those who had published a book on the subject, his was titled: **1975 in Prophecy!** When it did not bring the nuclear war he predicted, some accepted that within the text, he never said war would happen in 1975, he made it clear that the Bible could not be pinned down as to dates. But, the title just would not go away, and people talked about this failure and lost faith in his preaching and his denomination, the Worldwide Church of God.

This was the lead-up to the Feast of Tabernacles, and brought out the charts. During the feast that fall, there were several sermons that were illustrated with the symbols from the Book of Revelation, and the Book of Daniel.

During the summer of 1967, we had a visit from a family from Michigan. We grew quite close to that family, and visited back and forth quite a bit. This family was George Kinney and his wife Bernita. George Kinney was a mail man, he worked for the Post Office until he retired. They had two children, and arrived with their car pulling a fold down camper. They set that up in our yard, and stayed at our place for the weekend. It was a very enjoyable visit, as I said they were a pleasant family.

George was really interested in health foods, and it was as a result of his encouragement that my parents bought their first juicer. George was convinced that vegetable and fruit juice was a life saver, and he had a lot of anecdotal stories that illustrated how natural, fresh juices could strengthen the body and heal it. He loved carrot juice, and had seen miraculous response to drinking carrot juice, so he drank a lot of it. He drank so much, that his skin was markedly orange. In the summer, when everyone had some kind of tan, it was not remarkable, but in the winter, he just looked orange.

When we visited them, their house was the first house I ever experienced with central air conditioning. It was also the first time I saw wall-to-wall carpeting. We had to take our shoes off at the door. Their carpet seemed so soft and long, and was quite a cushion that we all enjoyed laying on.

In the morning, George made breakfast, and we had whole wheat pancakes with maple syrup, and fried hamburgers. When he served the meat, he said, "Try it with syrup on it, it is really good that way." I had eaten burgers with catsup and mustard, but never syrup, but I tried it and he was right, it tasted good. After we all finished eating, he informed us that we had just eaten goat meat. I had to agree, it was good, and tasted like good beef.

For many years, George and my father would call and talk to each other several times a year. Although the

Bethel Assembly and the Michigan Assembly went down separate paths after 1969, we at Bethel thought of the Michigan Assembly like they truly were our brothers. Sometimes you disagree, and sometimes you don't get along, but you still have so much in common that you are still brothers. I never felt animosity at Bethel toward the brethren in Michigan.

The Feast of 1967

The feast approached, and plans were again made to go to Jackson's Gap. We traveled there full of anticipation for a good feast. As we traveled around the bypass around Chattanooga, Tennessee, thr left front tire blew out. We were in the Ford Station Wagon, pulling a large, heavy, fold down camper. We were in the left lane, on a sweeping right turn when the tire blew out. I know that only my father's excellent skill at driving heavy loads saved us that day. He kept the car under control, and took it across three lanes of traffic with the flat tire safely. He changed it without incident, and we resumed the trip.

When we got to the feast, there was a different spirit there than we felt the previous year. There was an edge to the people that may have been from the Arab-Israeli War, or maybe there was something else. Maybe there was gossip circulating. Maybe there were bad feelings on the ground because they had begun selling lots to brethren and a community was forming with all those problems. I don't know what was at the root of it, but it was not the same. You could see there were hard feelings between some of the local families.

Shortly after the feast began, Elder Bob McBride taught the children's class, in the form of a Bible quiz game. Looking back, he did this for a purpose. Throughout the game, the Meyer and the Young children could answer any question that he threw at us, but the local youth from Jackson's Gap could hardly answer anything about the Bible. When he asked them questions from the pop culture (from the world, as he put it), they could answer almost all of those questions, and we could not. It was obvious that we spent our time in the Bible, and the local youth did not. I could see the resentment in the local youth from this game.

In services that night, he went on and on about the difference, and stressed that we must be careful, or we would lose the youth of the Sacred Name Movement to the world. What he did not think about was that all the kids from the north were upheld, and all the kids from the south were ridiculed. The next day, we all got invited down to the lake to take a walk, and off we went, as soon as we were out of sight of the house, they turned on us, and announced that they were going to beat up the smart Yankees. They said, "Maybe you won the war, but we will beat you this time." We turned and as a group headed for the house, and for safety, on the run. Thankfully, we were quickly back in sight of the adults, and they could see something was wrong as the local kids were chasing the visitors at a run.

Well, the local kids were all taken into the McBride house, and nothing more was said about the event. We were treated with sullenness by them the rest of the feast, but there was no love shown to us either.

About the middle of the feast, my father got a phone call from his boss, and he was told, "We need you back here... if you don't get back here now, you won't have a job. " My father told his boss that he was not able to leave; he would be home as scheduled. However, the rest of the feast, that provided another worry. What was he going to do?

After the feast, he went to work as usual, he was not fired, and not another word was said about it. Thankfully, he still had his job and worked in it for three more years.

Throughout the feast, sermons and Bible Studies concentrated on the role of Israel in prophecy. The general consensus in the Sacred Name Movement was that the Europeans were part of a literal Israel. It was generally accepted that the Western European nations and their colonies, the United States, Canada, Australia, New Zealand were all a part of the so-called Ten Lost Tribes of Israel.

The Oliphants, Kenneth Whitney and his wife, and the Lawton's were all there in 1967. Kenneth Whitney and his wife were from Wyoming, and were friends with the Mansager family. I believe that they drove the farthest that year to attend the feast.

Near the end of the feast, a sermon was preached about baptism, as had been preached the previous year. This year, there were quite a few new families, and some of them wanted to be baptized. As I recall, Mike Olyphant and his wife, and the Whitney's also wanted to be immersed. I was feeling very strongly that I wanted to make a personal commitment to salvation. I had just turned 13, and I got up my nerve and talked to my father about it. He asked me some questions, enough to know that I was serious, and then he consented to my baptism. Shortly after that, my brother Jacob also asked for baptism, and both of us were baptized at the feast of 1967 in the lake in front of the McBride's house.

Just before the end of the feast, I rode with Mike Olyphant into Jackson's Gap to get some food at the store for the kitchen. He parked along the street, and we went into the store about a block from his pickup truck. After we finished the shopping, I took the first bags to the truck while he paid the bill.

As I walked along the sidewalk, an elderly black man with a real pleasant demeanor came toward me, and out of deference and respect for his age, I stepped off the sidewalk. He stepped off too, right in front of me, and he quietly said, "Get back on the sidewalk, we don't want no trouble. If someone you move for me, it will go hard for me." I realized what he meant, and took the sidewalk again, and nodded appreciatively at him. But my heart was heavy. I never should have taken the sidewalk while any old man had to wait beside it with bowed head, for me, a child.

In that one moment, I learned about rascism and prejudice. Over the years, when I see rascism or prejudice, I feel a personal resentment and anger, and I confess it. My grandparents on both sides taught us that, "Red and Yellow, Black and White, we are precious in his sight." It may be a kids song, but the message is deep. Under that thin skin, we are not more different that any other men of diverse cultures.

From all around the world, who do I get along with the best? Farmers. No matter what color of skin, or language or culture, if I meet a farmer, we have a lot of things to talk about!

At the end of the feast, the Wilds family and their group from Texas and Oklahoma arrived again. This time they brought even more people. This time, they really stirred up the spirit. At the close of the feast, we learned that every month, the local churches had a special music night of priase and worship, and it was Pastor McBride's turn to host the night of praise. Several of the elders tried to reason with him not to bring in people singing in the "Pagan Names."

When the open song service came, about 50 outsiders came in cars, and services began. More than half the Sacred Name Believers stayed out of the service. They were all appalled, and kept asking, "Why is this happening?", "Is the Sacred Name important or is it irrelevant?" and, "Who is in charge of this group; who is keeping it on the straight and narrow?"

A lot of talk revolved around what is the role of a shepherd. Some of those who had gone into the service felt conscience stricken and left the service. This night of music caused great dissent and discouragement. The ultimate question began to arise, "Why are we here?"

This soured everyone, and many of us began to pack to head home. This question began to be asked at this feast, and "Who is in charge?" became what I would call the theme of the next year and a half. During that next year and a half, we heard of congregations in turmoil, marriages breaking apart, radical false doctrines being promulgated, and youth getting in trouble.

When a leader stepped forward and strongly reprimanded the offenders, then resolutions could be made, and the congregations were stronger. Somehow, after someone sinned, some type of repentance and change had to come to pass. If no leader stepped up, then the congregation seemed to go into turmoil. Each strong leader had to handle sin in their own way, but it had to be handled. I recall years later, someone came to my father and complained about how a Sacred Name pastor had corrected him in a wrong way for his sin. My father asked him, "Is there any right way to confront someone for sinning?"

These lessons greatly influenced the developments of the next several years. Although my father expressed strongly to us that all he wanted to do was to preach and evangelize, he also realized that leading a group of people may be thrust on him against his wishes. If the sheep have no shepherd, and if they are defenseless, should not the capable men rise up to protect and guide them?

I am not writing a comprehensive history of the Sacred Name Movement; this is only a record of my memories, what I personally heard and saw, and what I learned.

Of those histories that have been written, you will see that from 1967 to 1970 almost every group made changes, and most groups that grew saw a rise of young, strong leadership.

The Bethel Assembly Begins

After the feast, we began once again to worship in our home each Sabbath. One day, our copy of **the Sacred Name Herald** arrived, and my father was stunned. Earl Boyd had published a personal letter from my mother to Ursula in which she made some comments about the local brethren around Bethel. My father confronted her, "Why did you write this? Are you turning into a gossip? Did all the gossip at the feast influence you?"

My mother was sobbing by this time, and explained that she was responding to Ursula's letter where she asked about the spiritual condition of the local brethren. She did not view answering the question asked of her as gossip. What she had written was simply a summary of how the local people may have had a lack of dedication, in that they made no effort to assemble for the Sabbath. She didn't realize how it would look to others if it was in print, out of context.

My parents immediately got in the car, and drove to the homes of the brethren involved, and they apologized for the letter. By following Matthew 18 quickly, they made peace with the brethren. However, I do believe that it made the brethren think about the lack of local services, because shortly after that, Jacob Bicher and Titus Eberly came to visit and talked about starting local services.

On the property of Titus Eberly was a small house that was empty, and could be used for services. By Passover 1968, arrangements were made, and services were begun. The families who had once met at Hamburg, 12 miles away, all reassembled, along with others who had learned the truth since 1963.

Publishing Truth

During this time, the contributions and the correspondence to the Assemblies of Yahweh office was growing. My father was spending more and more time answering questions. He began to have my mother type up the radio messages on stencils and run them on a mimeograph machine to make copies, and then he would send them out to answer questions.

So, if an inquirer asked about the holidays of the Bible, he would send them a message on the feast days. If they asked about clean foods, he would send them a message on Leviticus 11. Some of the recipients of these messages began to pressure him to bundle them into a magazine for convenience, so that the messages could be shared with those who could not hear the radio broadcasts. Thus began the magazine, **The Sacred Name Broadcaster**. Published every other month at first, it was run off on the mimeograph, and assembled on our kitchen table by hand and hand stapled.

The first copies were sent to only those who requested them, and were hand addressed. Quickly, the magazine was advertised on the radio broadcasts, and very quickly, a mailing list was begun. To address the magazines, metal address plates were made by a printing company in Lebanon, Pa, and were used in an addressograph machine set up in the corner of our living

room. I will here include the description of the
Addressograph machine from Wikipedia:

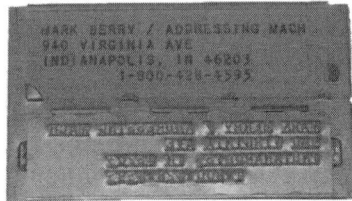

An addressograph machine of the 1960s was essentially a steel
frame with an integrated keyboard for stamping out address plates, a
cassette-style plate feeder, a heavy-duty, rapidly moving inked
ribbon, a platten for hand-feeding the mail piece, and a foot pedal for
stamping the address. The individual steel address plates were
inserted into card-sized frames which had a series of slots along the
top where colored metal flags could also be inserted for sorting
purposes. The plate assemblies were placed in steel cassettes
resembling library card catalogue drawers, which were manually
inserted into the machine. At the press of the foot pedal the plate
assemblies were swapped in sequence in a similar fashion to a slide
projector, placing an impression of the raised type onto the mail
piece.

I include this description, because so much has
changed. Addressing mail today is so different.
Computers store and addresses with ease. The addresses
print with ink-jets onto removable sticky Avery labels.
With the Addressographs, you printed right on the
mailer. A drawer of steel plates only held about 250
plates, and was very heavy. Today, a flash drive the size
of your little finger can hold millions of addresses.

At this time, the one wall of our living room became a printshop. The mimeograph machine was first, the a saddle stapler, and then the addressograph. It was hard to get past them to get around to the back of my father's desk. Behind his desk was the typewriter and a small worktable. He had to move his books out into the center hallway.

After about three hand-assembled magazines, a printer was engaged to commercially print the magazine. I believe the first magazine went out to 144 homes. Soon, the mailing list was over a thousand.

Competition and Jealousy

This brings us to the next development in the Sacred Name Movement: Envy and Jealousy. We began to have sudden drop-in calls from Elders and leaders from around the country. They wanted to see for themselves what was going on at Bethel. As we used to say, "The Rumor Mills are Grinding Away." While at the feast, everyone wanted the message to go out, but when it actually happened, people panicked. People began to imagine things, make up stories, and to gossip. This gossip got carried all around the country, and created a dilemma for some who heard it. They felt the need to prove if it was true of false.

The first visitors were from Morton. At that time, they were publishing **the Faith** Magazine. They stopped by one Sabbath for a visit, and we had a very nice visit, since we hadn't seen them for about a year. Later that winter, we heard that the **Faith** Magazine was moving to Michigan because they did not want my dad to get control of it. The fact was that **the Faith** Magazine was moving to Michigan, the gossip was that they didn't want my dad to get control of it. Such is human nature, mix fact with gossip, and stir up trouble. My parents didn't regard any of this talk seriously. The purpose of **the Faith** and **The Sacred Name Broadcaster** were different, and they always have been.

This summer a girl from Albany, NY, came to visit with us for a couple of weeks. Her name was Jeannie Rosenberg. We visited with the Rosenbergs a few times. The last time was in the winter of 1968, and they had a real severe blizzard the weekend we were there. We children stayed in their camper in the yard, and it was sure cold!

Another visitor that summer was Lillian Tompkins from Denver, Co. She moved to Pa to help with the work, as the work load was getting too heavy for my parents. She was a retired secretary, and she stayed a couple of months to help out. While she was there, I saw a help wanted ad in the local paper for the restaurant, Midway Diner. I asked my father if I could get a job, and my father was very upset. She calmed him down, talked him through it, and encouraged him to allow me to take the job. I applied, and worked there all through High School.

Chapter 8

The Feast of 1968, in Michigan

The brethren from Michigan invited us to come to Michigan for the feast. The Bethel Assembly decided to go to Michigan, and so did some of the members of the Pittsburg Assembly. An assembly had grown up in Pittsbugh led by Willie Young and Sylvester Anthony. They were also young men, full of zeal, and they worked diligently around Pittsburg to spread the Sacred Name truth. At this feast, Donald Mansager attended with his wife Mildred. They were baptized at this feast.

Most of the Michigan members were there including: the Sam Graham family, the George Kinney family, The Lloyd Parry family, the Richard Francis family, Donald Trowbridge, and Earl Bigford. I believe that Kenneth Whitney was also there. Don and Mildred Mansager came to the feast with a big Airstream camper. I was amazed at the cleverness of the Airstream company at putting so many nice features in their campers.

Overall, it was an inspiring feast, but one service stands out in my memory. During the feast, a visitor stood up to preach, and spent the whole sermon preaching against keeping the feasts. We were all puzzled. "Why come to the feast if you believe the feasts should not be kept?" And why insult everyone that did drive so far to attend, by telling them they were wrong?

This raised the question again, "Who is in charge?"

Maybe that is not a question with merit, but it sure became important when the feasts were disrupted by commotion, by false doctrine, by disagreements, and by conflicts. Where was the peace of Yahweh? Where was the unity of the brethren?

As stated in **The Faith** magazine, "The assembly of Yahweh which puts out **The Faith** does not consider itself to be any denomination, but is made up of small groups and individuals around the nation, each completely autonomous." This structure began at this time to be questioned. Although this structure was historic, history also proved that under that structure, growth was not occurring.

I remember sitting by my father at a picnic table outside when Donald Mansager came and sat with us. He began to talk in depth about what he was seeing, as a first-time observer at a feast. He expressed dismay at the confusion of doctrines he had heard at this first feast. He discussed with my father how any business could not prosper without proper leadership.

They discussed how the Sacred Name Movement tended to let the spirit lead and control things, but they also discussed how in the Bible Yahweh worked through men to lead and teach. They agreed that something had to be done, and Don Mansager pressed my father to organize his followers into a group and to be the leader.

He said, "You are a natural leader, the people respect and follow you. The Broadcast is bearing fruit. You can build that ministry into a group of dedicated people who are taught truth, and who will work together to accomplish great things!"

Later I realized that this was Don Mansager's nature. He would push another man forward, and then work in his shadow, supporting him but not taking the lead himself. My father was very close to Don Mansager for many years. What happened between us in 1980 will be told at some other time, not here by me.

High School

I entered High School in 1968, and decisions about my extra-curricular activities had to be made. Clearly, we were not allowed to go to any dances, because dancing was such a worldly activity. They dance in bars and get drunk. We did not want our children to turn into sexual perverts and drunks, so no dancing.

Back in 1963, when we were studying with the Jehovah's Witnesses from Schubert, they used to bring their high school aged son along, and sometimes we went for walks. On one of those walks, he asked us if we danced. Of course, we did not. He hummed a few songs, and showed us how to do the frug, the mashed potato, and the twist. Kid stuff to be sure, but I learned that my feet loved to move and to dance. I will blame him for that propensity throughout my life!

We could not play in concerts on the Sabbath, so no Friday or Saturday concerts with the band. We could not play with the band on Saturday games, or even at band competitions. It put pressure on the band director when we did not show up. It isolated us from the other players.

I wanted to be involved in sports. I could run and run and run, so I tried out for track. In 1964, Jim Ryun had broken the four minute mile, and I admired him for that. I lived a mile from the restaurant where I worked, and after work, although I was tired, I would run home. As the months went by, I began to turn on the steam, as they say, pushing myself to a faster and faster pace. I never could jog, like most runners. I was not super-fast, but I was much better than average.

So, I wanted to be on the track team. I was the first sibling that wanted an extracurricular activity, so this opened new discussions at home. When I asked my parents, they had to disuss every angle. Was it worldly? Were the little shorts they ran in, immodest? Did they have meets on Friday night or Saturday?

My parents decided that I could be on the track team, so I was on it for four years. I ran the mile and half mile, and threw the discus, and the shot put. My friend,

Glen Eberly, also in the Sacred Names, also joined. My brother Jacob joined the track team·two years later. Since the soccer teams and the football teams used the buses on Friday night and Saturday, the track teams in our county had their meets on Tuesdays and Thursdays.

In my Junior year, I was invited to districts at Reading, and the meet was on Saturday. I was not able to go. And then, at the last minute, my father took a trip to Pittsburgh, the services were cancelled at Bethel, and I realized I could sneak away that day. So, early in the morning, I got on my bike, and rode eight miles to school, got on the bus, and rode to Reading. That day, I was wracked with guilt. Of course, I had burned a lot of energy riding my bike eight miles to school, and my heart was also not in the competition, because I knew that my family would not have supported my running. I dropped out of the race at the beginning of the fourth lap, and told my coach I had cramped up.

I never ran a race on the Sabbath again.

The Spring of 1969, Assemblies of Yahweh

In the spring of 1969, plans had gone forward to organize a religious group under the name of Assemblies of Yahweh. While other groups were local, this group from the start was intended to be international, thence the name, "Assemblies of Yahweh," as a central headquarters for congregations all over the world who would choose to affiliate with Bethel. It was not arrogance that formed the group, it was logical and simply a way to organizationally recognize what was happening.

There were actually serious discussions about 1973 with the Elders as to whether the headquarters offices should be separated from the Bethel Assembly, so that people would better understand that ALL congregations, including that of Bethel, were joined voluntarily in this effort. Elder Mansager, as I recall raised the question, and was supported by Elder McFarland. However, it never was done, because it was felt overall, that although there would have been visual benefits from the separation, Yahweh put this together as it was, and we should not tear it apart.

True or not, that was the discussion and the decision that led to the Bethel congregation and the Headquarters to be so intertwined. It also contributed to the split of 1980 in big part.

The first part of the process to getting the Assemblies of Yahweh incorporated was to hire a lawyer to prepare the paperwork. Today, so much is done online, the process of 1969 seems archaic! Bylaws and Articles of Incorporation were drawn up, and heavily edited to be in conformance with the Bible. The attorney made all the changes and the organization paperwork was filed in Harrisburg. Later on, about 1971, it was discovered that the IRS c3 could not be granted because a few words in the Articles of Incorporation had to be changed. That was done, and from that point, the legal position was secure.

As this process was being undertaken through the spring of 1969, Elder Meyer typed up the notes he had been preparing for six years about his views for requirements for religious practice. He titled this, "The Statement of Doctrine." For several months, we used this as a framework for our services, so that the brethren at Bethel could ask questions about the doctrines, and the language could be refined and become precise.

When the Statement of Doctrine was complete, Elder Meyer re-typed it personally on Mimeograph stencils, and sent copies around to all the Elders and dedicated members for their comment. At the same time, he planned a trip to go all around the country, to discuss the organization with the leaders of the Sacred Name Movement, and to get their blessing. Throughout his life, although he led, he wanted to feel a consensus of opinion behind him.

He left on that trip, as I recall in June, after school left out, and he headed south. He was driving the 1964 Station Wagon. That car had a big 352 ci engine, and drank gas. But, when gas was about 39 cents per gallon, it didn't matter. He swung through the south, visiting every assembly he knew of, big or small, and discussing with them the Statement of Doctrine and Assemblies of Yahweh.

His trip took him through Texas, and he told the story of how one afternoon, he was barreling along a straight, smooth, two-lane cement road heading toward New Mexico, and he looked down and he was doing over 100 mph. He was stunned. He had no cruise control on that car, and the smooth, straight road gradually deceived him into thinking he was still doing 65 mph. That car was never the same after that trip, probably due to that long stretch of high speed.

He continued west, and turned up the California coast, and up through Oregon, and then turned east, through Idaho, Colorado, up through Wyoming, and then he headed for Chicago and Michigan. He ended the trip as he came through Pittsburgh and then home.

The consensus to his face was very supportive. Later on, he was puzzled that so many in the Sacred Name Groups held back and did not join with us.

However, and here I interject my interpretation, gained over 40 years of experience and observation of events, there were several factors at play:

First) a natural suspicion of organizations of any kind.

Second)   a fear that some of the language in the documents would overrule their local leadership at some point

Third) A fear that Elder Meyer was setting himself up to be over them in all matters.

Fourth) A fear of loss of local autonomy

Fifth) A fear of loss of local contributions to Bethel

These seeds of dissent planted in 1969 grew and bloomed ten years later in the split of 1980.

With a feeling of consensus, and with changes recommended by brethren all over the country, the final draft of the Statement of Doctrine was printed at the printer

Chapter 9

The Feast of 1969

Elder Meyer believed that he had the momentum of an organization behind him, and the support of the brethren that he visited. The brethren had encouraged him to hold the feast there at Bethel. The brethren all began looking about, as the meeting hall could never hold the feast. Someone suggested Brightbill's Grove, and it was engaged for the feast.

The meeting hall was just a picnic pavilion that was enclosed, and there was a large grove of old trees around it that provided shade and a sedate environment. In the end of the pavilion, there was a simple kitchen area. The sides of the pavilion folded down for hot days, but could be easily raised on cold days and at nights.

The brethren came with their campers; some of them stayed at Motels, some of the brethren stayed at home. There was no pressure to conform, there was freedom of expression and choice, just like we had seen in the Sacred Name assemblies at other feasts.

Many brethren from other, older assemblies attended the feasts of 1969, 1970, and 1971, 1972, and 1973.. Only about 1974 did we see a distinct separation form between the Assemblies of Yahweh at Bethel, and congregations within that organization, and the other assemblies of the Sacred Name movement.

The biggest difference at this feast from previous feasts, was that there was no disruption. The Elders had decided to only allow speakers that they knew, and that had been proven. If someone was to speak, it was understood that they would not raise controversial doctrines with the intent to divide. This is not to say that every message toed a party line. No message outlines were collected and approved. The Holy Spirit was in control, and peace reigned throughout the feast.

Because of the most recent publication, the subjects of all the sermons and sermonettes were the doctrines we needed for salvation. This was a huge difference from other Sacred Name groups. Most groups did not have a creed of any kind, and the doctrines were fluid. After this 1969 feast, it became common for an Elder to create his own creed, and to use that to lead. It was a whole new era.

Right or wrong, the creation of this carefully crafted attempt to outline and define all the doctrines a believer should follow, changed the Sacred Name movement. I saw, over the years, this Statement of Doctrine change with time. Usually, after a confrontation or attack from outside, the leadership would re-examine the document, and make revisions to make it more clear, and to avert future issues. Also, after a major sin would be revealed, especially if it became a public disgrace, then the doctrine at play would be re-examined and clarified to avert sins and embarrassments like that in the future.

After the split of 1980, for example, a whole section on the subject of government was spelled out and added. This effort to clarify the government structures was actually begun in 1979, before the split. I know, because I still have my research cards on which I recorded all my research. Due to my research in the winter of 1979 into the history and basis of early apostolic assembly government, I was asked to give a presentation to the ministerial board in the spring of 1980. This research was added to, and codified into the "Government in the Assemblies," addition to the statement of doctrine.More about that later.

During this time, we were still living in the old farmhouse along Rt. 22 east of Bethel. The work was still primarily done there, although some of the mailings were carried to the meeting hall. As the mailing list for the Sacred Name Broadcaster was growing, it was becoming impossible to do that mailing in our home. This need, through the winter of '69 into the spring of '70, became more and more evident, that the Assemblies of Yahweh had outgrown our house, and an office must be acquired.

As this talk began to circulate, jealousies again arose, and were certainly evident in the feast of 1970.

Bible Class in School

With my open observance all through school, I got a lot of questions from teachers and other students. I was marked as the Bible expert in class, and I carried my Bible with me every day. I had bought a Companion Bible in 1968, and with all the notes and appendixes, it was like carrying a small library! Because I carried my Bible, others in my classes began to carry theirs, and we soon had impromptu Bible Studies in school. This led to a teacher suggesting that we form a Bible Club. He told us that he would be proud to be the supervising teacher. His name was Mr. Wentling, and he was a sincere Christian. We went to the principal, and got permission to have the club every week during study hall.

This was during the time that prayers were being taken out of schools. This is when the Atheists were suing municipalities to get rid of religious symbols. Our school was very conservative, and they seemed proud that the students had arisen to make a stand for the Bible. In the club, we invited speakers in from various churches, to tell us about their congregations, and their beliefs and practices. My father was invited in to speak in the club. Since he was there, my social studies teacher, Mr Scarpignato, also invited him to our class for further discussions. He and my father got along great, and he actually came to the Assembly offices at least once for further discussions with my father.

Chapter 10

The Feast of 1970

The first thing I heard from the visitors at the 1970 feast was a complaint that the Bethel feast was too far for people from the Midwest, and from west of the Mississippi River to attend. I hear this numerous times from various families.

Secondly, there was a strong push for the Assemblies to have an office. Several of the leaders were talking about moving the offices to Missouri, because that would be more central. However, many of the brethren sitting around the lunch tables and throughout the grove, agreed that Yahweh had put the office at Bethel. Again, whether that should have been a determining conclusion, it was a strong argument. Who can argue with Yahweh?

So, the discussion turned to what was available for rent or purchase? Several of the families were staying at the White Hall Motel, and they were told that it was for sale. Elder Mansager spoke to my father about it, and my father asked them to check it out. He wanted to stay a bit remote from it, as he sensed that there was jealousy brewing and fears about his leadership being ego driven. He knew what was being whispered about, and he tried his best to avert it.

When Elder Mansager came back with the report, he was totally convinced that this was the right place for the offices, and it had living quarters that the Meyer family could live in to act as caretakers for the grounds and to keep a presence on the property for security sake. My father was still worried and skeptical. "Was this really Yahweh's will?" He kept asking. Like so many religions, a lot of time is spent trying to figure out what Yahweh wants us to do. Even though we have free will, in the Sacred Name movement it is commonly held that Yahweh has our lives all planned out, and if we are careful not to upset the plan, our lives will be blessed.

Almost all of the men at the feast piled into cars and made a visit to the motel. After the tour, my father was convinced. At the next service, announcements were made about what was happening with the office situation. The elders had a ministerial meeting, and it was unanimous that the motel office idea should be pursued.

Although the feast of 1970 had serious undercurrents of suspicions and doubt about central leadership, the idea of buying an office invigorated everyone, and drew together the brethren in a unified commitment to work together to accomplish this great goal.

This became a learned lesson, and at almost every feast, a new program was broached. It kept the people focused toward a goal, and took attention off the individuals. The new program required contributions, and promised great rewards in evangelism. The programs also distracted the gossips. It was a win – win idea for all feasts. Please don't take this as a criticism. I have always been a student of human nature, and it fascinates me to see how administrative decisions and directions affect people in the administration and outside of it. These are my observations and conclusions. You may differ.

Also at this feast, the complaints about the distance from those such as the Mansager's and Whitneys and those from Texas was heard, and plans were made to investigate places to hold the feast in the center of the country.

My parents were members of AAA, and I saw my parents poring over the AAA travel guide for Missouri, as they studied the state to find a suitable campground to hold the feast. Our experience had proven that the people who lived at the feast site felt more included, and became closer to the brethren. Those who stayed at home or in a motel, were more isolated, and remote in every way.

So the criteria looked for was a campground out in a wilderness area, some distance from a population center, but near enough to mass transit that people could come to the feast by train, bus or plane. Cuivre River State Park seemed to be a good candidate, and plans were made for my father to fly out to St. Louis, rent a car, and investigate several sites.

That winter was busy. After the feast, the owner of the White Hall Motel made it his business to sell the Motel to the Assemblies of Yahweh. He and his wife were splitting up, and he wanted the sale to go through urgently. He tried everything to be congenial. He even brought candy and treats for the children, and he took us all out for ice cream. With all the negotiations for the Motel, and the plans to go to St Louis to scout for a feast site, my father was busy. The sale of the Motel went through, and with the obvious urgency of the seller, the price was quite advantageous for the assembly.

The White Hall Motel, just after the purchase by Assemblies of Yahweh. To show the concern with symbolism, it was discovered just as the purchase was complete, that the building had the shape of the Hebrew Dalet, which represents an open door. That confirmed that it was Yahweh's will that this be the office.

About that time, Titus Eberly sold his property at Shubert, and the assembly started to hold services at the Strausstown Fire Hall. The Eberly's moved to a farm in upstate Pa. Glenn Eberly was a senior at that time, and he stayed in the Motel during the end of his Senior year and he helped in the offices and in the printshop. We had weekly services there at Strausstown until the Motel renovations made space for services to be held in the Motel.

The trip to St Louis was successful, and Cuivre River State Park was selected for the feast. We rented Camp Derricotte for the main camp, and had access to Camp Frenchman's Bluff for extra kitchen space and cooler space. Camp Derricotte had a large kitchen, a sufficient mess hall to be used for services and meals without tearing down and setting up for every meal, and a number of cabins the brethren could stay in. Also in the park was a ball field, tennis courts, and a nice lake for baptisms.

Along with everything else, we had to do renovations at the Motel to prepare for moving the offices, and we had to move the family. My mother used this opportunity to go through everything, and we had a huge bonfire of all the furniture, clothing, and junk that she did not want to drag along to the Motel. The fire burned all afternoon into the night, and the local police was called to see what the fire was. There was no trouble, but he cautioned us against burning again at night. My father's brother, Carl, had a pickup truck, and he did most of the hauling for us.

Explosive Growth around the US

With the move to the Motel, we began to have regular visitors from the Sacred Name Movement. Quite a number of people thought since we had a Motel there at Bethel, that they could just move in and get free housing for helping out around the property. The rooms on the north side of the Motel were rented out for the first year, to help pay the mortgage, and the west wing was used for offices, so there were no freebie rooms for those who wanted to invite themselves to stay. As soon as the growth guaranteed that the mortgage payment could be made, the motel rooms were phased out.

Meanwhile, strong indications came from California that there was a group of former members of the Worldwide Church of God who wanted to join the Assemblies of Yahweh. At the time that the Motel was purchased, Elder Meyer was also hired full time to run the office. The growth that year was superb, with new inquirers and income growing steadily. It was obvious that there would have to be help very soon at the office.

Several times that summer, and into 1971, my father traveled to California to teach and organize a California assembly. He also traveled to Canada that year. The brethren at Bethel renovated the center rooms of the Motel to make a meeting hall, and the pews and the piano from Irvington, NJ were moved in, and we began having services there on the Sabbath. However, the feasts had begun to be held at the Shartlesville Fire Hall because we needed more space. Below are some pictures of the services held at Pentecost, 1971, in Shartlesville.

Lunch at services at the Strausstown Fire Hall, probably at Pentecost, 1972. Elder Jacob O. Meyer is in the center. My sister Mary and John Pederson, her husband stand at the far wall under the clock.

Lunch, the same day. Loading up that plate is me, the author. Notice, kids, my thick curly hair, now long gone! On the very left, you can see my uncle, Landis Deck, who just passed away this year.

Elder Meyer and Russell Goodale. Russell was an engineer from Virginia, who was very fluent in technically proper Spanish. He helped to publish some of the Spanish literature.

The group photo, Pentecost, 1972

If you look closely at the group picture, in the middle row, from the left, the second person wearing sunglasses is Henry McFarland, one of the brethren from California. He was a legal assistant in the office of Elder Herman Hoeh of the Worldwide Church of God at Pasadena. He had graduated from the college that Armstrong had founded, Ambassador College with high honors.

Henry McFarland was assigned to be sure that the Sacred Name Movement was not infringing on their trademarks or copyrights. He had to examine the material closely, and he began to read the literature coming from Bethel, and became convinced that the Sacred Name was imperative.

As the California assembly grew, Jean Rockhold joined the services there also. Here in this picture, near the front, is her daughter, Jill, standing beside my little sister Rachel, and holding my youngest brother, Nathaniel by the shoulders. The Rockholds and Henry McFarland flew in for the feast. Later, the next spring, Henry McFarland, Tim Haworth, and the Rockholds all moved to Bethel.

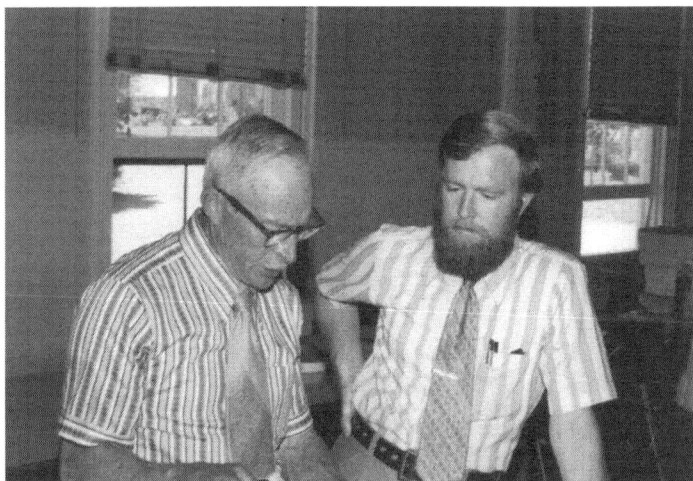

Henry McFarland and Russell Goodale discuss the Bible.

During this time there was explosive growth in Assemblies of Yahweh meetings all over the country. The radio broadcast was bearing fruit, and the publications were focused entirely on the simple message, "What must I do to be saved." As the congregations quickly grew, dissent also grew, as people brought in many ideas and doctrines that were conflicting. To bring peace, **the Sacred Name Broadcaster** began to run various articles defining even further, doctrines of all kinds.

Up to this point, the published articles we teaching the most obvious of the doctrines. As dissent occurred, other doctrines that often are given to various interpretations began to be taught, and many who had begun to assemble with us, drifted away.

I include these pages about the Assemblies of Yahweh growth because of two reasons: at this time, the divide between the Assemblies of Yahweh at Bethel, and the rest of the Sacred Name Movement had not yet formed. Every time we had a feast, we had visitors from other assemblies around the country, and they were welcome.

The Doctrines Change

Gradually, as the Assemblies of Yahweh added more and more teachings that were required for baptism, we were more and more different than the Sacred Name groups. Remember, at this time, most of the Sacred Name groups did not even have a required written creed. They allowed the holy spirit to police their ranks. As the Assemblies of Yahweh defined more and more doctrines, we had less and less in common with the other groups.

At this time, there was a strong push to attempt to purify the language. You will notice from about 1972, that words began to drop letters in the Assembly publications. We pushed back against those who wanted to purify the English language by removing all the pagan-related words. But still that line of which words to allow and which to restrict kept moving.

I preached a sermonette about that time that explained that the Greeks had 20,000 deities, and many of those deities names were parts of our language. I had learned that the early Greek culture did as so many others still do today. To teach the language (especially the noun meanings) stories are attached to each word, and this living dictionary becomes eventually interpreted as a religion. So the words really preceded the pagan interpretation, and we really should not worry about that connection.

Besides, how far will you go? Once you head down that road, you could eliminate the majority of our language! Some replied that we should change to Hebrew. This argument for ridding English of pagan names and their connections was a ridiculous argument, but it hung on to some extent to this day. The unique letter-dropping format made the Assemblies of Yahweh look more and morecultish.

From the early 1930s, as people studied, they learned, and changed their spelling for Yahweh's name. The Sacred Name Movement is and always has been composed of those that have been in the truth for a while, and those who just learned the Sacred Name. This forms a blend of doctrine from the past with doctrine just introduced. The doctrinal state of the Sacred Name Movement is truly fluid, and always has been. The efforts to nail down that doctrine, and affix it, were not unique to the Bethel publications.

A New Talmud

I had a long talk with Rabbi Shertz from the Harrisburg Orthodox Jewish Congregation about the Talmud. He was fascinated with the Assemblies of Yahweh, and asked many questions about how we got so many "Christians" to adopt strict Old Testament practices. As we talked, he asked why we reject the Talmud. I explained that we stuck to the written Bible, and did not introduce men's writings to our studies.

He responded that every church writes a Talmud. I was puzzled. He explained that every Bible verse is open to some interpretation, and as soon as you begin to discuss the Bible, people differ on interpretation. So, when that gets written down, it is a new Talmud. So, he asked, "Why write a new Talmud, when we have one that goes back 2,000 years?"

That was an eye opening moment. Ever since then, I regard all magazine articles and books as part and parcel of a new Talmud. It led me to go back to the more simplified, major doctrines, and to believe that everyone should study and make up their own mind about the rest. This put me at odds with the rest of the leadership of the Assemblies of Yahweh.

Other groups arose around the country of all types. Some were very local, and some were regional. The Assemblies of Yahweh was the only one that was truly international, and so, many references by onlookers labeled Elder Jacob O. Meyer as the leader of the Sacred Name Movement, and this offended leaders of other congregations.

In addition, because members were drifting to other Sacred Name groups from the Assemblies of Yahweh, mention of the other groups became less, and when mentioned, they were ridiculed for "false doctrines and confusion." This was designed to discourage the brethren from seeking others outside of the the Assemblies of Yahweh.

I noticed about 1978, that as I read over the publications from the other Sacred Name groups, that most of the other groups were now comprised of people I knew. They had been meeting with us, or had left us.

Of course, the official story was that they had "sin in their lives," or they were "confused in doctrine." When you say that, you no longer have to maintain a relationship with them or the other groups, and it all seems so tidy. Compare it to a divorce, when the relationship gets hard, just throw it away and cut all ties.

Shortly, it was being published that the Assemblies of Yahweh was not even part of the Sacred Name Movement.

Shunning

In the early literature of the Sacred Name Movement, there is no discussion of shunning. Instead of throwing people out, they were trying to bring them in. That kept them so busy, they did not worry about what to do when things got hard to administrate.

Gradually, as the groups grew, various forms of congregational discipline were adopted by various leaders. Shunning became rather popular about 1979, and caused the split of several of the Sacred Name groups.

Matthew 18 is all about solving problems in a congregation. The passage begins (vs 1-10) with admonitions not to offend anyone by word or deed. Then, vs 11-14 encourages us to seek out those who stray. Verses 15 20 explain how we can solve problems. And the passage ends with the parables of forgiveness and tolerance.

Gradually, to maintain order, brethren were taught that it was an obligation to withdraw from those who were disorderly. Shunning was not done by only one group. Every group that grew in the 1970s and 1980s engaged in shunning to some extent.

"Now we command you brethren, in the name of our Sovereign Yahshua the Messiah, that you withdraw yourselves from every brother that walks disorderly, and not after the tradition which they received of us." 2 Thess. 3:6

This was applied not only to those who were stirring confusion, but even to those who were confused about doctrine. Instead of being tolerant and waiting for the spirit to resolve issues in the hearts of those seeking truth, people were quickly tossed out of the groups. Sometimes those rejected were totally confused as to why they were no longer welcome.

Shunning became a hammer, beating people and driving them away from the Sacred Name groups. People felt victimized by such behavior, and scars were left. For me, this was a stunning change. From the 1960s, when everyone was welcome, often to the detriment of peace and order, to the 1970s, when peace and order were to be maintained at all costs, no matter who suffered.

Remember, I am not pointing this description at any one group. There were more than a half dozen groups that established strict rules, and guarded their doors. Several groups in the south had their ushers begin to carry concealed weapons for defense. This was outrageous. To live in fear to attend a church service; to live in fear of former members is outrageous.

Of course, there were many causes for such fears, for as the doctrines got stricter, and rules of admission got strict, some marriages broke apart, people in the group remarried, and the severed spouses were understandably angry. Custody issues erupted, and all the other nasty elements of broken homes.

This is the seamy underground of the Sacred Name Movement. It is not spoken of openly. I trace it all back to the obsession of the rule-makers, as I call them.

In every organization, there are people who crave more rules. They want things nailed down. They personally need clear definitions, rules of conduct, and strong directions from a leader. So, they pressure for more rules, more doctrines, more enforcement.

The more that doctrines are developed, and new interpretations are published, the more enforcement that occurs, the stricter the government, the more often these offenses occur toward the sheep.

Instead of opening the doors to admit all who are lost, troubled, and seeking a home, the doors are guarded, and the sheep are chased away. It is easy to only bring in people you like, because you can label all the others as goats or black sheep.

On a personal level, members learn that if they displease the leader, there will be consequences of some type. This is what causes so many to accuse religious groups of emotional abuse. When a leader is upset, the consequences can range from an expression of displeasure as subtle as a huff or a snort, to a personal confrontation either private or public.

Sometimes, members are called out during sermons or testimonies by act or even by name. Some leaders require a public confession of sin or transgression for offenses to individuals or the creed.

The bottom line is that if you don't want to lose your church, your family, or your place in the community, you will toe the line, and conform in every way to what is expected of you. This causes a person to live in fear of transgressing a rule, or contradicting an interpretation, or even making a mistake.

Shunning has become the one doctrine that has changed the Sacred Name Movement the most, and it is the one doctrine that has caused the Sacred Name Movement to stop growing. It is clearly divisive. I never heard a visitor describe a Sacred Name group as paranoid until 1978. After that, I heard it a lot. The shunning doctrine leads to paranoia in the membership, and the leadership. Paranoia is easily detected by a visitor, and they don't want to come back.

Chapter 11

The Feast of 1971

In the early summer of 1971, Elder Meyer used my almost new Maverick to make a journey around the U.S. He published reports of that trip, so I won't repeat it here. That trip, however, was the last trip that crossed the lines between the Sacred Name groups and the Assemblies of Yahweh. After 1971, we would travel within 10 miles of a Sacred Name congregation, and not stop by for a visit.

I found this to be sad. Not only did we not stop, if we even talked about stopping, we were regarded as potential traitors to our own group. The divide was now formed.

During that trip, many services and Bible studies were held with new inquirers, and it led to the biggest Sacred Name east every held in the U.S. to that point. We rejoiced when 140 people gathered at Camp Derricotte for the Feast of Tabernacles. At this same time, the Worldwide Church of God had a total feast attendance of close to 20,000. I just throw that fact in here for comparison. Sometimes we all need a reality check!

That group of 140 was from all over the U.S. Many of the attendees were leaders of groups whose members could not attend. This is the cost of a single central feast. I would estimate that at that time, there were over 5,000 people around the country who could not travel due to health issues, job issues, family issues, etc. To travel across the country and take off two weeks of work, is nearly impossible for the average family.

Arguments were made then, and still are made, that we must sacrifice. We should do whatever it takes to keep the feasts. But, I asked then, and I ask now... why must we have one central feast? The decisions made in the Sacred Name movement for central organization and central feasts did set the Sacred Name Movement down one path, but it may not have been the best path.

Sacrifice. That seemed to be the message of the feast of 1971. Give up whatever it takes for salvation. True, to a point. However, it is also true that some families lost their jobs due to going to the feasts. Some even lost their homes because of it. Many families became impoverished due to trying to observe the doctrines as published.

Immediately before the feast of 1971, the woman hired as cook quit. My father had flown to Missouri to prepare for the feast, and we were going to follow him about three days later. As soon as he got to Missouri, he called the cook, and she told him she could not make it. He immediately called my mother and they decided that we would do the kitchen planning and direction. I was working as a cook in the local diner, Midway Diner. I had a good grasp of portions, large-scale cooking and many recipes in my head.

My mother and I sat down and devised a menu, and then began to make a store list. Thus began my three years as kitchen manager at the feasts. After 1973, we no longer provided a central kitchen for the feast, encouraging the brethren, instead, to camp and have their own family cooking at the feasts.

As I stated before, central meals were nice, but they took so many brethren away from services and cost so much money for the group. Discontinuing the central meals was a good idea.

One group that attended this feast was the prior Holiness group from Mississippi under Pastor Clyde Wilson. We became very close to this group, and they were very active in the Assemblies of Yahweh. Besides the Wilson's other families from that church included the Jordan's and the Cupit's.

The Print Shop

At this feast, a momentous decision was made to purchase printing equipment and to do our own printing. I was approached by the Elders to see if I was interested in doing the printing. I agreed with excitement. I had enjoyed working in the print shop of Earl Boyd, and I love the graphic arts. To learn the printing trade and to work with photography, typesetting, printing and binding was all positive for me.

For the Assemblies of Yahweh, having their own print shop lowered their costs, and gave them the ability to greatly expand their publications with little extra investment.

Elders in 1972 at the Feast of Tabernacles: Donald Mansager, Clyde Wilson, Jacob O. Meyer and Roger Meyer

Senior Year in High School

In my senior year, I did not shave, and the little hairs on my chin and cheeks kept growing. Halfway through the year, I had a pretty well defined beard. One day, the principal stopped me and said, "Young man, you better shave that off." I looked him straight in the eye, and said, "I better have my father come in and talk to you about that."

The principal did a double-take, averted his eyes, and walked away. He knew my father had a big flowing beard, from when he had visited the school for Bible Club. He never said a word to me again about the beard.

This was during the time of the rebellion of youth, and boys were always trying to push the boundaries with long hair, mustaches, and beards. I was the first to get away with a beard, and after that, about half the boys in school had a mustache or goatee or beard. Some of the boys grew long hair, and we called them "Sue," after the Johnny Cash song. It was an interesting time.

The schools today far different than they were back then!

By the end of the year, graduation plans were being made. There were three Sacred Name Believers in 12th grade that year. Bethel had a good-sized assembly by this time, with about 100 persons meeting every Sabbath. My aunt Mildred, and her husband, Landis Deck were attending pretty regularly, and my cousin Margie was also a senior. So, Glenn Eberly, Margie, and I were set to graduate. However, in the meantime, the assembly had raised questions about the cap and gown. Should we wear the cap and gown? Books were brought out about the black robed priests of pagan religion, and the origins of the symbols.

It may have been a stretch, to compare a graduation to a priest of baal, but the connection was made, and so we could not wear the cap and gown. We requested the ability to wear proper suits and dress for a formal occasion, and that request was denied.

So, after consulting with an attorney, we filed suit to enjoin the school to allow us to wear formal attire instead of the cap and gown. We lost that case, and were not allowed to sit on the stage with the other seniors. We could not go on stage to pick up our diplomas. We had to sit in the audience, and our names were not read, and we had to pick up our diplomas in the office from the principal after the ceremony.

Many justifications have been given in the Sacred Name movement for all kinds of strict observance activities and decisions. One of the most popular is, "For thou art an holy people unto the LORD thy God, and the LORD hath chosen thee to be a peculiar people unto himself, above all the nations that are upon the earth. " Deut. 14:2

Whether this means what people say is not the point of this reference, it is just to explain why these types of separation from the rest of the culture are done. The people who use such verses really want to stand out.

They exult in seeing their women in ankle length skirts, with arms and necks covered, and huge white veils on their heads. Some Sacred Name groups require the men to wear long sleeves all year, to wear a large yarmulke, have flowing beards, and with fringes applied by some formula some man made up.

This is the same issue that the Jews have stuggled with. The Jews have the Ultra-orthodox, the Orthodox, the Modern Orthodox, the Conservative, and the Reformed. Each one of the orthodox groups can be recognized by their clothing. The Sacred Name believers struggle with this same approach.

Others argue that the USA is a Christian culture, since polls show that over 75% of the Americans say they believe in the Bible and worship occasionally. Some Sacred Name believers say we don't need to drive huge wedges between us and them.

As Christians, the rest of America is like our close cousin. We disagree on some things, but in most moral decisions we agree. On a day to day basis, we can walk the streets, and we look, act and talk like everyone else. Why create huge wedges and impediments between the Sacred Name believers and the rest of the culture? Are we trying to drive them away?

Attempts to bridge the Divide

The publication of **the Sacred Scriptures, Bethel Edition**, was momentous. Since the publication of the

Bible by A.B. Traina, no other Sacred Name Bible had been done. The Bible that Traina put out had lots of issues, but even after his death, it was not corrected. For over a decade, my father talked of printing a Bible. Finally, in 1980, the technology had gotten to the point that this was feasible. We could produce the Bible, and sell it at cost.

As that Bible was at the press, the question was raised, will we sell to the Sacred Name Movement? At first, the answer was emphatically, YES! Then, about 1985, the rule makers began to push for restrictions. I argued strongly that we should feed all who are hungry. That we should be the leaders in disseminating truth without restriction.

Others argued that we put in the investment and time, and they did not, so why should we provide it to them so cheaply? (Sounds like the Little Red Hen story…) That argument prevailed.

However, I confess that for about 10 years, as Office manager, I was sneaking shipments of Bibles out into the Sacred Name Movement. I had a co-conspirator in Vivian Offerdahl, the secretary, who felt as I did that we should provide truth to all. One of my favorite channels was to Sam Graham. We shipped him many cases of Bibles and wrote up his checks as donations. We got caught in 1997, as I recall, and there was a storm in the office over it, and I was ordered not to send any more to him. I still feel the criticism was well worth it, and still feel that we should have freely provided all literature and Bibles to every group around the world who needed it.

In 1984, I pressured my father to begin to re-open communication with the Sacred Name Movement. It was during the legal battles we had with the elders who split off from us, and much gossip was circulating about these suits and why were pursued them. The two of us visited many of the old congregations that summer, and re-established communication for a short time. However, my goal was to re-open the doors and work together as we used to. When others found out what my goal was, I received more criticism.

The Sacred Name movement had begun a Unity Conference every year, and I pushed for us to attend that conference, and with four or five of our elders, really help to bring peace to the Sacred Name Movement. This idea was totally rejected and we never went. While a few of us were pushing for peace, there were others working to cause interruptions and interference in the Sacred Name Movement, and to raise strife.

Do you remember how Paul raised a commotion and saved his own life in Jerusalem when he said was on trial? This method of causing confusion still works today, and had often been used in the Sacred Name Movement.

"When Paul perceived that the one part were Sadducees and the other Pharisees, he cried out I the council, Brethren I am a Pharisee, a son of Pharisees: touching the hope and resurrection of the dead I am called in question." This caused such a disruption in the council that Paul was spared.

In the Sacred Name Movement, this divisive tactic is often used. When the pressure comes on a person, often they raise a divisive doctrine, and cause confusion. I won't list all the doctrines that are commonly argued over... because every doctrine has strongly defined beliefs and those who side with one opinion or the other.

A clear formula to avoid this strife has never been agreed upon. There are ways to bring peace, but as long as there are those who want strife, there never will be peace in the Sacred Name Movement.

Disclaimers, etc

As they say, "Opinions are like noses, everyone has one." I know that there will be those who disagree with my conclusions in this book. That is fine. Actually, it should be welcomed. I believe that we learn from adversity, and we learn from discourse. If this book opens up discourse on these subjects, then, may Yahweh be praised.

Some will look for faults in my accounts. That is fine. If there are errors of name or place, please inform me. I can be reached at trail.riders@aol.com if you wish to communicate with me.

If you don't like my conclusions, well, that is why we have freedom of religion in America. We have free will, and free expression, and can speak our minds and opinions under the first amendment. I enjoy that privilege, and rejoice that you can too.

I won't get involved in debate, but if you want to speak your mind, pro or con, email me. I have spent over 50 years as a Sacred Name Believer, and I can assure you that I have heard every argument on every doctrine. Where I am and what I do now in my life is the result of thinking on my own, and making my own decisions.

I read once that Daniel Boone was chastised by his sister for not going to church, and he wrote back to her that he does all his study and worship at home, quietly, with his Bible on his knees. I believe that for some, that is a good practice, when you are looking for peace.

My father, Elder Jacob O. Meyer passed away in 2010, and all of us gathered for his funeral. Below is a picture of my mother and her ten children.

Quite frankly, my father should have written this book as he certainly remembered and was involved with these events and people so much more deeply than I was. But, he is gone, and if the story does not get written

.

now, soon it will totally be lost. I invite others who lived this time to write their stories so they are preserved.

Back row: Daniel, Micah, Jacob, Nathaniel, Solomon, Jonathan, Joseph. Front row: Rachel, Mary, Ruth F. Meyer, Sarah.

If you just want to share your story, or tell me if this book helped you… email me. I welcome them. Of course, some of you lost track of me years ago, I welcome hearing from you too.

And, for those with pictures of the old days, send them to me! I would be happy to relive the memories… and may Yahweh be with us all in these troublous times.

List of Illustrations

10793746R10099

Made in the USA
San Bernardino, CA
27 April 2014